The Diary of Nina Kosterina

Translated from the Russian by Mirra Ginsburg
THE DIARY OF NINA KOSTERINA
AZEF by *Roman Goul*
THE MASTER AND MARGARITA by *Mikhail Bulgakov*

Translated from the Russian and Edited by Mirra Ginsburg
THE FATAL EGGS AND OTHER SOVIET SATIRE
THE DRAGON by *Yevgeny Zamyatin*
LAST DOOR TO AIYA (Soviet science fiction)

The Diary of
Nina Kosterina

Translated from the Russian and with an Introduction

by Mirra Ginsburg

CROWN PUBLISHERS, INC., NEW YORK

Introduction

Nina Kosterina began her diary in June, 1936, at the age of fifteen. The last entry, made on the eve of Nina's departure to fight as a partisan in the rear of the invading Germans, is dated November 14, 1941.

Not intended for publication, the diary conveys a great sense of spontaneity and warmth. In some ways it is reminiscent of the diary of Anne Frank. Both girls lived in periods of intense crisis, both were vital and strong personalities, with an overwhelming desire to live, both experimented, each in her own way and within the limits of her situation, with their first friendships and their first loves.

In scope, this diary is necessarily wider. It is both a remarkably moving personal document and a revealing record of life in Soviet Russia during the period of the great purges, trials, and terror which consolidated Stalin's rule. It also provides a vivid glimpse of Russia during the early days of World War II.

According to her father, a journalist who supplied an afterword to the diary when it was published as a book in Russia (in 1964), Nina was born in 1921, when both her parents were members of a partisan unit in the Civil

War. She spent much of her childhood in government creches and Young Pioneer camps, and shared in all the difficulties of the first postrevolutionary years. "When we were demobilized," writes her father, A. Kosterin, "we had only our army coats, one change of underwear, and a desire to work and study."

Nina's first cradle was a trough. After that she slept on two chairs, and, for the rest of her life, on an iron army cot. Her first shoes were made by her mother from her father's old partisan jacket; her first dresses, from her mother's blouses and skirts. Her first doll was a homemade rag doll made by her mother.

As the diary opens, Nina and her family (and you know and like them immediately) are on their way to vacation near a small town on the Volga. Warm, gay, and carefree, they take long boat trips, spend nights around bonfires, singing, laughing, and listening to the father's recollections of the early heroic days of the Revolution and Civil War. Further entries record the return to Moscow, Nina's school days, her activities as a member of the Young Communist League (Komsomol), her friendships, her emotional crises. They tell about the gathering wave of terror; the arrests of acquaintances and friends, her uncles, and, later, her father; the reactions of her family; and her own efforts throughout all this to grow and to build her life. They record her feelings and her comments on people, books, art, music, theatre, and, most of all, her stormy personal relationships.

The daughter of a Communist, Nina goes through all the stages of a Communist upbringing. She is active in the various organizations for children and young people. As a Komsomol member, she helps in elections, works with groups of Young Pioneers and the even younger Oktyabryata, or Children of the October Revolution. She dutifully reads the prescribed political tracts—Marx, Lenin, Lunacharsky. She is horrified at the "revelations" of the "Trotskyite trials," and wonders how old revolutionaries like Bukharin, Radek, and others could have become "enemies of the people."

Yet, despite this general mold, Nina remains an individual. The larger political events of her time intrude upon her life, but her chief preoccupations are intensely personal. She is deeply involved with people—with her family and her friends. She reads a great deal, and her reading largely reflects her own emotional choices—within the scope of what is permitted and hence available.

At a time when individual problems and relationships are being expunged from literature, and all new writing is being reduced to the "industrial" theme, to eulogizing "socialist construction" and serving the interests of the party and its objectives, Nina reads nineteenth-century writers and poets, and also contemporary European writers whose works are admitted to publication in Russia. Intensely romantic, she often quotes Goethe, Heine, Lermontov, Fet, Koltsov, Nekrasov, and the more recent Blok, Mayakovsky, and Esenin.

Despite her political activities, she seems to be essentially little concerned with politics. There is never any overt political criticism. Nina witnesses the expulsion of schoolmates from the Komsomol (and thus from any hope of a future) because members of their families have been arrested and they refuse to renounce them. Her own father, uncles, and aunts are arrested. Old friends abandon the family. She herself is rejected by the college of her choice. Nina suffers, but never pins the blame for what is happening on anyone. There seems to be an almost deliberate paralysis of the critical function. The conditions of her life are given conditions, and she lives within them. When the pressure of events becomes too overwhelming, Nina plunges into more and more work in order not to think. Yet stirrings of doubt and questions begin to break through. In the end, there is tacit knowledge that her father is not guilty (and, by inference, neither are many of the other victims of the mass terror). She feels increasingly Russian and increasingly proud of Russian history. She thinks of her ancestors, of her father and uncles who were declared "enemies of the people," and asks: "How can I, their daughter in flesh and blood, believe this?" And when war breaks out and the invading Germans "slice into" Russia "like a knife into butter," Nina feels that her place is at the front. She volunteers for duty as a partisan, leaving the man she loves.

Both in what the diary touches on and in what it omits, it provides enormous insight into the mentality and functioning of the Russian people, and into Russian life at the time. But above all, it is a warm and absorbing story of the growing up of a very attractive human being. For the main theme of the diary is life itself—life which asserts itself in spite of the harsh and rigid terms imposed upon it by the dictatorship. The theme is universal: it is Nina's search for growth, for knowledge, for a direction in living, for integrity in relation to herself and to others, for friendship, and for love. On the eve of her departure for the front, she writes: "I want so much to live, to work, to create. . . . To live, to live!"

The diary is followed by two short letters of farewell from Nina to her mother and younger sister, who had been evacuated from Moscow. The father's whereabouts are unknown. Desperately lonely on her last days in Moscow, bombarded and feverishly preparing for possible siege, Nina writes: "I have a single thought: perhaps my action will save father?"*

The final item is a short letter from the army, notifying Nina's mother of her daughter's death in action in December, 1941.

Nina Kosterina's diary first appeared in Russian in the Soviet monthly *Novy Mir* in December, 1962, twenty-one years after Nina made her last entry.

MIRRA GINSBURG

---

* A grimly ironic twist was added to the fate of the Kosterin family by the expulsion of Nina's father from the Soviet Writers' Union for signing various protests, in 1966 and 1967, against the arrests and persecutions of writers insisting on freedom from Party supervision.

First Copybook
[1936]

June 20

Exams are over. I am an eighth-year student! And suddenly, out of nowhere, came the feeling—I shall keep a diary. Said, and done. But what shall I call it? I thought about it for a long time. I began to ask myself: Who am I? What am I? I have no talents of any kind. . . . And, thinking of how untalented I am, I decided to call my diary "The Diary of an Ordinary Girl." Completely ordinary. I don't even dream of anything special. Other girls dream of becoming doctors, engineers. To me, the future is utterly hidden, in a fog.

I want to begin my diary with a date that is most vivid in my memory. It was April 8th, my fifteenth birthday. I gave a party, and my guests were Alik, Boris, Volodya, Volya, Lusya, Tonya, and Vitya. Before the party, I was terribly nervous, afraid that everybody would be bored. But the evening went beautifully—I've never had so much fun at a birthday party. Also, this was the first time that I "ventured" to dance with boys—with Alik and Vitya. When Alik put his arm around my waist, and

I put my hand on his shoulder, a shiver ran through me —it was such an exciting and happy feeling. I have been dancing for a long time, I love to dance, but I have never enjoyed it so much before. Alik was fooling around and lifted me up in the air. My heart stopped, I could not catch my breath, and my cheeks flamed. . . .

Afterward we played forfeit games, and Alik and I kissed. The first time, he kissed me; the second time, I kissed him, when he was saying good-bye. We also played "flirt of the flowers." Volodya and Lusya turned it into a flirtation between themselves. I did not like the game and stopped playing. There were other games too. Everybody stayed late, until eleven o'clock.

It was a good party. It reinforced my friendship with the boys, but cooled off my relations with the girls. Ogloblina was especially angry and later called me a "toady." There were many arguments about that, and finally she was transferred to another class.

The May Day celebrations were very gay. We marched in demonstrations across the Red Square; I saw all the leaders. We sang, danced, shouted. . . . And in the evening we went to see the operetta *The Bird Seller*. I loved it.

I must also tell about the visit to the Museum of Fine Arts. I went with the whole family. But in the museum I went off by myself: I wanted to see whatever I felt like, and to look at it as long as I felt like. There were many things I liked, but best of all was a certain French painting: a seacoast, ships in the distance, beautiful, branching trees on the shore, and a crowd of people stretching their arms toward the sea in panic and despair. There was also an English painting—a woman in a gray dress, with a riding crop in her hand, standing on a veranda.

But the conclusion I drew from this visit to the museum was that I must go again, and next time with a guide.

Now I must make a record for myself of the important events of this period: Gorky died, and a draft for a new Constitution has been published. The Constitution is something I understand very little, although I feel that this is an event of great importance to our country. But Gorky's death was like a personal sorrow to me. We have his complete works. I've read many of them, and some stirred me so much that I could not sleep. And now, Gorky is gone. . . .

There was also a lot of anxiety in connection with my admission to the Komsomol. I have, generally, been reading the newspapers, but all the same I had to go to father for help. He talked to me for two hours, reminding me about many things and explaining others, especially about the Constitution. After the talk with him, I went to the District Committee of the Komsomol quite calmly. What a father I have! There were ten of us at the District Committee, and everybody was nervous. I did not like the District Committee office: dirty, with smudged, dingy walls, nowhere to sit down. It seemed to me that I was calm, but others said that I came out of the office white as chalk. They gave me a membership card, tiny-tiny, white.

At home I showed it to papa. He caught me in his arms and threw me up and kissed me. "Good girl, Ninok!" He said it in such a way that I was filled with joy and pride.

Oh, yes, I almost forgot about something that applies to us women: publication of a draft law to forbid abortions. One evening I read reports by three Polish women about life in Poland, where women give birth to their babies right by the machines they operate, in the marketplace, in ditches . . . I was so upset that when I went to bed I buried my nose in the pillow and burst out crying.

Let me list the books I have read lately. I read Kochin's *Peasant Girls*. I liked it very much. Hugo's *The Man Who Laughs* almost made me flunk the physics test—I got so absorbed in reading, I forgot that I had to prepare for the exam.

During examination days I went twice to Kamerny Theatre and saw the movie *The Circus* three times. Orlova is marvelous!

During exams, papa made a promise: if I did well, we would go to Khvalynsk. Yesterday was the last exam—geography. I passed. I've graduated from the Seven-Year School. Hurrah, we are going to Khvalynsk!

June 22

I am writing in the train. I'm traveling with Uncle Ilyusha. Mama and Lelya left earlier. The windows in our compartment do not open, and it is suffocating. I took the upper berth—it is more convenient for reading and . . . dreaming! I read over the letters from Nastya, my Khvalynsk girl friend. They're nice, but so many mistakes! My letters must be full of them too.

June 26, Khvalynsk

We have no ink and no pen, therefore I am writing with a pencil.

We arrived in the morning of the 24th. I didn't sleep all night—was standing in the prow of the ship and looking at the Volga. Darkness, wind. Small clouds racing in the sky. Among them, stars flashed and disappeared, and there was something troubling and mysterious about it. And beneath, in the darkness, the menacing noise and plashing of the Volga. . . . Nothing but two lights ahead —red and white—and between them, the ship rushing headlong through the stormy, tumultuous night.

As soon as I came, I changed and hurried off to see Nastya. Stayed with her all day, then decided to remain for the night. We climbed into the hayloft, and talked and talked till dawn.

July 7

I'm giving too little attention to my diary! I reprimand myself for it!

Nastya and I are almost inseparable. We talk about everything. We recall last summer, discuss the news, which I tell her every morning, talk about our future.

The days are hot. Papa spends all his time on the banks of the Volga with his fishing rod. Quite often, he takes us along. Once we spent a night on an island, around a big fire. Papa made a tent out of sheets, but just before dawn a violent wind came up and the tent collapsed. There was a lot of noise and laughter, but mama was angry. "A lovely outing," she kept saying. And we looked for firewood in the dark again and rebuilt the fire. And papa sang songs.

We climbed up the mountains too and found a ruined chapel in the dense woods. What a beautiful view opens up from above on the mountains and forests! And what delicious water in the springs!

August 2

Again an interruption in my diary. But here in the country there is no desire to write at all, especially in this heat. The pen simply drops from my hand.

Our main diversion is bathing. We splash around in the Volga two or three hours on end, until our teeth begin to chatter. Today I went to the island with Nastya and Yadya. Just as we went in to swim, we stepped into a hole and immediately got our lungs full of water. We jumped out from under, and Yad'ka began to scream, but I shushed her so furiously that she stopped, and only her eyes bulged with terror. We barely managed to get back to shore. Yad'ka called me her savior.

August 3

When I went to bed last night, I remembered how we started drowning, and it sent a shiver down my back. Especially Yad'ka's eyes—horribly, unbelievably huge!

Papa dragged us off again to fish from a rowboat. We rowed far upstream. Papa caught two carp and a pike perch. We had a pail with a fire in the boat. Mama made fish soup—delicious! I don't remember a tastier one in my lifetime.

Then we were caught in a downpour and got wet to the skin. Only Lelya was saved; papa covered her with his coat. We came back dripping but happy.

Papa said that on the way back we'll travel until Saratov by rowboat. I hate to leave, but papa is implacable. I feel like crying, but it won't do any good.

August 16

Letter to Nastya

My dear friend Nastya!

It was only yesterday that we returned to Moscow. Ten days since we said good-bye. I'll tell you in order all about our trip.

When the boat slid away from the bank, I felt so miserable, I didn't know what to do. And I kept wondering: how was it that we did not even kiss in parting? And why do I have this persistent premonition that we shall never meet again?

The boat glides noiselessly, and your dear figure recedes into the distance. . . . I wave and wave with my handkerchief, and can scarcely keep back the tears. When you disappeared, I could not take my eyes away from the beautiful Khvalynsk mountains. Those mountains and that city had become like home to me. Then we came to the harbor where we had disembarked six weeks before. Papa bought a large can of beer, and we went on. This was my last look at Khvalynsk.

New impressions came pouring in. In our little boat we felt with especial force the mighty expanse and beauty of the Volga. On the right, forested mountains. Papa told us ancient legends about them. But most of all he spoke about the Civil War. The Volsk and Khvalynsk regions saw the most furious battles. I love to hear papa speak about those days— what a time it was! Our days are also interesting, but they are somehow too "tidy," too "proper." . . .

We camped for the night on a deserted sandy beach. We made a fire. And in the morning we went on. A high wind rose during the day, and the Volga went wild with storm. I also took up oars, but papa and I could barely keep the boat going against the wind. Lelya shook with fear, and her eyes were like Yadya's when she was drowning off the island.

In the end the wind forced us to come ashore and take shelter in the bushes. By evening it calmed down, and we resumed our journey. The night came, pitch black. Nothing but lights here and there on the river. Papa knew what they were and rowed confidently. Suddenly there was a steamboat ahead, and another behind us, catching up with us.

Both mama and I thought that they were coming directly at us. And Lelya crouched at the bottom of our boat and whimpered, "I'm frightened." Papa calmly and unhurriedly went on swinging the oars and grinning. Mama demanded that we draw up to the shore. And papa asked, "Are you frightened

too, Nina?" I admitted I was. It was only then that
he turned aside, toward shore. But we could find no
firewood in the dark and were attacked by millions
of mosquitoes. We managed to stretch out on the
floor of the boat, and covered ourselves with sheets.

During the day we were again fighting the wind,
which raised such huge waves that our boat was lost
among them. But papa rowed so skillfully that not a
drop splashed into the boat. . . . Nevertheless, we
did not reach Volsk and had to spend the night in
the woods again. We found shelter in some shack,
and the night was magnificent. Again we sat around
a fire, and papa was telling us about the Civil War in
the Volga region and the Caucasus.

In the morning we approached Volsk, but the
wind rose again. I was also rowing and did something wrong. The boat swerved sideways into a
wave and it broke over us. Papa was furious and
swore at me. We had to return ashore and dry out.

It was only in the afternoon, when the wind
fell, that we finally reached Volsk. I liked the city;
it is noisier and busier than Khvalynsk. We bought
provisions. Papa got himself a supply of vodka and
beer, and biscuits and candy for us. We went for a
swim nearby. The coast was very good, dropping
steeply at once. But I was not afraid. And papa, in
the boat, kept teasing (after a swig of vodka!) that
I was afraid of depth.

We spent the night not far from Volsk. At night
the wind rose and blew down our makeshift tents.
We sat till morning by the fire. In the morning we
discovered that sand got in our candy. But Lelya
and I cleaned it up a bit and ate it anyway, disregarding the sand grating in our teeth. Papa and
mama had a good laugh when they found out.

During the day we passed Voskresensk. Here we
had another adventure: the steamships going by sent
up such huge waves that they swept over our boat

and all our things got wet. We had to dry ourselves again and pour more beer for papa.

That day we approached Markstadt, a German town. We camped further down and spent an uneventful night around a fire. Papa cooked a wonderful gruel. Then we drank lots of tea and sang songs.

Next day we came to Saratov. As we were drawing up to shore, a motorboat sped by and hit a swimming boy. You should have heard him screaming, Nastya! But he did not drown, he was rescued. People said afterward that his arm was torn off together with his shoulder.

We spent two days in Saratov, sightseeing. It's a fine city, big and beautiful. I was especially impressed with the public park. They call it "The Lindens." Masses of flowers, greenery, shade, fountains.

We left Saratov by train at four in the afternoon, and were in Moscow the next morning!

And so ended our journey. It was lovely, but I missed you. Especially in the evenings by the fire, or when the boat moved quietly amidstream, and wooded mountains floated by, and thoughts of you. I wondered what you were doing then.

There is no one in Moscow, and I've nothing to do. I long to see you and . . . to kiss you! What a pity we did not kiss good-bye.

Nastyusha, start a diary. Then all your memories will stay vivid. And send me excerpts from your diary.

What a long year ahead! And I have no desire to study at all.

Write very soon, Nastya, I miss you. Damned paper—you cannot express on it one hundredth of your heart's longing. . . . If we could only be together, what happiness that would be!

Yours till my dying day,
NINA

August 19

Yesterday I had an unexpected call from Volodka. We talked for half an hour. And in the evening, movies: Charlie Chaplin's *Modern Times*. I liked *The Circus* better.

August 31

The other day Volodka came to see me. I hate it when boys come to visit me. Everybody at home gives me such looks afterward that . . . Oh, to the devil with them!

Today I went to school and met many of the kids. Our group will be broken up into two. All the teachers are new. Even the number of the school was changed.

September 5

September 1st we had a demonstration. We fooled around, danced in the streets in the rain. Tired ourselves out and got drenched. But it was fun. . . .

I was chosen monitor. I am so afraid I won't be up to it. Even in bed at night I think of all sorts of class business.

September 6

I received a letter from Nastya. . . .

Last night I went to an evening at the Institute of Law. I met Zhenechka, our former Pioneer leader. I think she has grown prettier. The girls talk about her because she uses lipstick and eyebrow pencil. And has a permanent. But I think there's nothing wrong with it. Zhenya has been married for a whole year. She is going to school and will be a lawyer.

The People's Commissar of Justice spoke. Then there was a concert, and later we danced. There were five of us, and therefore one would remain every time without a partner. But I danced all the time. At the end I was so tired I almost dropped in the middle of the dance floor.

We went home at two in the morning. I was so happy and excited after the evening that a militiaman in the street asked, "Why are you laughing so much?" And I said, laughing, "I feel good, so I laugh!" On Nikitskaya I met a group of students. One of them looked at me and cried, "This is the girl I'll go home with!" I laughed, and the students kept shouting, "Take me, take me with you!"

I came home late. It was lucky papa was out, or I would have gotten a scolding. At home I glanced into the mirror and liked myself (which happens seldom)—red-cheeked, eyes burning, gay . . .

September 9

LETTER TO NASTYA

HELLO, MY BELOVED NASTYUSHA!

I have not written for a long time, I've been up to my ears in all sorts of activities. I was chosen to be monitor on the very first day of school, even though I did not want it. But I am a member of the Komsomol and cannot refuse social obligations.

Dear Nastya, the first thing I saw when I opened your letter was the flowers. Thanks! As I look at these little flowers from the Volga, I shall always think of you. And I have your picture before me. I look and look at it, and cannot have my fill. And I remembered that you don't have mine. I shall try to get some snapshots soon and will send you one.

Don't be offended, Nastya, but I am not pleased with your letter. Not because it is so short. You must have hurried, and therefore made many mistakes. Your description of your trip to Kuybyshev is too skimpy. I would very much like to know what the city is like. These are your faults. Write me about my faults too. Will you?

It is not pleasant to be monitor. You always get it from the teachers for poor discipline, and from the students for trying to improve discipline. It's lucky that all the "old-timers"—from my previous class—are behind me. The new students are terribly full of airs. At the next meeting I will resign. I've had enough of it.

And now the main thing: papa is going to the Russian Far East for two years. It takes a whole month to get there. First by train, then by boat. It has not been decided yet, but the whole family may go. I am both eager to go, and afraid: I may fall back in my studies. And I will not see you for two years.

I am waiting for your letter. I kiss you three hundred times.

NINA

September 21

Hello, dear diary! I have neglected you altogether.

Too much runing around. Now I am not only monitor, but also chairman of our Komsomol squad. Our organizer is Mulka, a very nice fellow. We have five members and three candidates. Of the eight, three are girls, one an empty-headed little coquette.

Our leader will be Lusya, from the Institute of Law. Chubby on the outside. What she's like inside remains to be seen.

We are not going to the Far East. We shall remain in Moscow. Papa will go alone.

September 23

Was at the Tretyakov Art Gallery today. We are taking up *The Tale of Igor's Host* at school. We stepped in to see the exhibition of Repin's paintings too. I loved his "Barge Haulers." I recalled papa's stories about our great-grandfathers who also walked along the riverbank towing barges. I must go to the gallery again.

September 30

A new member has been added to our family—another sister. Mother gave birth at the hospital last night. Everybody expected a boy. Grandmother is very disappointed.

We have a new kitten too. Everybody loves it.

October 7

We argued for a long time about a name for our new sister. I wanted her named Natasha, grandmother insisted on Olya. Mama won and named her Vera. Oh, but she is a noisy brat, our Vera—she got used to being held and howls all the time.

My Komsomol assignment is to work with a group of Oktyabryata. I haven't started yet.

Vera was given a bath tonight. She seemed to love the water. And didn't give a peep when she was being dried. Lelya and I are wild about her. We kiss her so much that she gives out little grunts.

October 20

We saw papa off today. He even shed a tear or two before starting on his long journey, and everybody's eyes were wet.

Yesterday papa bought me a guitar. I was so happy I threw my arms around his neck and wouldn't stop kissing him. Such a pity he had to go. For two years now we shall be without the companion of our frequent surprise outings in the country, which father was so clever at thinking up. A fire somewhere in a clearing, shashlyk roasting on the coals. For himself, he would bring some vodka, for us—a soft drink. We'd eat the half-raw bits of meat—they smelled of smoke—wash them down with a drink, and start singing, "Glorious sea, sacred Baikal . . ." Mobs of people came to our house these past few days—father's friends and colleagues.

Now I am sitting and strumming the guitar. I have already gone through four lessons in the instruction book.

Yesterday we had a Komsomol meeting. Mulka reported on his work as organizer. A committee of three was elected. My assignment to work with the Oktyabryata group was confirmed, despite my fervent refusals.

November 4

On the 2nd I attended a district meeting at the Institute of Law. The secretary of the District Committee gave a talk. I came home at two in the morning.

For the first quarter I have the following marks: "fair" in algebra and physics, "excellent" in physiology, and "good" in everything else.

During the last six days before the end of the quarter, we had tests every day. I'm all worn out. I've even developed insomnia and headaches. I cannot wait for the holidays—we'll have three days.

Nastya doesn't write, and I don't know what to think. The guitar hangs on the wall, silent—I have no time.

November 7

At last, the holidays! We'll have some fun now!

Last night I was in a dreadful mood, I don't even know why. I cried all evening and wanted to die. I fell asleep in tears. But today everything is singing inside me. I jumped up early, feeling marvelous. We had tea with grandmother's cakes. Then off to school. Stayed there until eleven, then went to the Institute of Law. The students were no longer there, but we managed to find them later in a kind of dead-end block off Hertzen Street. We sang and danced for an hour and a half to the music of an accordion.

At two we went to Red Square. I saw Stalin. There was some confusion beyond the square. We were caught in a crush in a narrow street and were swept along. Lidka, naturally, started screaming, and we shouted at her. When we were dragged out to a wider street, things eased up, but the militiamen blocked the way and began to force everybody into a wide detour. Suddenly we heard cries, "They broke through, they broke through [the militia chain]!" . . . We rushed there. The militia were pressed to the wall, everybody was running, and we ran with them.

In the evening, Sima came to pick me up. Stella and Lelya pestered us and we had to take them along. First we went to Arbat Square, where the children's exhibits were. In all the show windows there were marvelous models of the Artek Children's Sanatorium, of characters from Pushkin's fairy tales, and so on. Mobs of people in the street. From Arbat we sent Stella and Lelya home, and went on to the Manege, where they'd built a stage and a platform for dancing. We looked at the stands of the food industries, then we wanted to dance, but there was too much of a crush. We went on to Theatre Square. I liked Stalin's portrait, about as big as the Mostorg Building. On the way back we stopped off at the Manege Square and danced our fill. I came home at eleven, with aching feet.

November 9

End of recess. The three days flew by in a flash. Yesterday Stella, Lelya, and I went to the zoo. There was a funny incident. Admission is a ruble and ten kopeks for an adult, and twenty-five kopeks for a child under twelve. I bought, correctly, two children's tickets (for Lelya and Stella), and one for an adult. Stella warned that they would not let her in on a child's ticket, she's such an overgrown kid! But we tried, and sure enough, they wouldn't let us in. We had to buy another adult ticket, but we had many laughs kidding her about it.

December 30

FIERY GREETINGS TO MY BELOVED NASTYA!
I received your letter this morning and read it in bed. You can't imagine how glad I was the moment I saw the envelope. I waited for your answer so long, and now it turns out that our "excellent" mails are so efficient that I never received your two letters.

My father is working in the Far East. Our darling sister Vera is already three months old, and she laughs beautifully. I do not know whether we'll join father. It is very cold there, and mama is afraid. It's dreadfully far, on the Sea of Okhotsk. But I would love to go—I want to see the world.

I am doing well at school and seldom get "fair." I am very active in the Komsomol. I am squad chairman and I lead an Oktyabryata group. I wear a Pioneer tie, an ICY* badge, and a red star. Our school is large, but there are only seven Komsomol

* International Communist Youth.

members, and so we get a heavy assignment load. But then, we have lots of prestige, too.

Dear Nastya, you must be bored in your provincial little town, and here life is so gay and exciting. We had marvelous times during the October celebrations and Constitution Day. I always dance so much that my feet are sore for a long time afterward. We often visit the Institute of Law (they are our patrons). * They always have a band. We are going there today. And tomorrow we'll all have a party at school. Where will you celebrate New Year's Eve? See that you have a good time! I am never without a partner and never miss a single dance. But with boys I dance very seldom—I am too embarrassed.

Recently we had a terrible blizzard. I was just going to school with one of the boys, when suddenly there was a blast of wind and whirling snow. We ran, but it was still far from school and we ran into a gateway to wait a while. The blizzard didn't stop. We were afraid we'd be late and ran again. We could not see anything two steps away; we had to hold each other by the hand. The wind was blowing so violently in our faces that we had to walk backward. We walked and laughed, and came to school all covered with snow. After this adventure, I was in an excellent mood.

Today is the first day of vacation. Last night a group of us went to the movies. We saw *The Goalkeeper of the Republic*. It's very good. On January 4th I am going to the theatre (Vsevolod Meyerhold's) to see *Woe From Wit*. From the 5th to the 11th, four of us (two girls and two boys) will stay at a rest home near Moscow.

* In the Soviet Union, one institution or enterprise often assumes "patronage" over another. The "patrons" supply their "protégés" with entertainment, books, and equipment, and generally maintain friendly contacts with them.

You must have heard that Nikolay Ostrovsky died recently. We went to see him in his coffin. He died at the age of thirty-two. Did you read his book *How Steel Was Tempered?* If you didn't, read it. It is a marvelous book.

Verochka just woke up and will probably start bawling. She is a good baby, everybody loves her. She laughs so hard, as if she understood things.

I have many girl friends at school, but my best friend is Lena Gershman. We sit at the same desk.

We are decorating our tree. We made lots of toys, bought twenty-five candles, beads, shiny balls, and so on. We shall also go to parties at Stella's and Irma's—they're our cousins.

I have a pretty new dress, blue, with a white collar and white belt.* I'll wear it today. They also bought me high-heeled slippers and new stockings. Now I am considered a young lady. Our Lelya has eczema. It is spreading to her face. She is as skinny as ever.

Nastyusha, answer me as soon as you get this letter.

I kiss you a million times.

Good-bye,
NINA

[1937]

January 25

I have neglected my diary—my first entry this year. Briefly, about January: the twelve days of vacation

---

* There is a sketch of this dress in colors in the diary.

passed very pleasantly, although I did not go away to the country. I often go to the skating rink, and also to the theatre. During January, I saw *Woe From Wit, The Marvelous Alloy, Princess Turandot* and *Floridsdorf*. Schoolwork is going badly. To heck with it, I am tired of school. . . .

The second Trotskyite trial is going on now. Frightful revelations. All of them will probably be shot.

January 31

Our poor kitten died. She wasn't given a chance to live, somebody poisoned her. And we don't know who could have done such a vile thing. She was always so gay and playful, but the last few days she vomited and did not eat. Yesterday Lelya and Margarita went to the doctor. He gave them a medicine, but "kitty" died before it came.

I remember the day we brought her home. She was so tiny, so helpless! All she did was lie on her yellow cushion. Such a darling kitten! The whole house is sorry now. Yet, when we collected money for the doctor, all we got was eighty kopeks. The rest—to make up the three rubles—came from me and Lelya. We contributed our entire savings.

February 7

The terrible trial is over. Of course, they will be shot. How could it have happened that old revolutionaries who had fought for decades for a people's government became enemies of the people? . . .

At school, things are picking up. We play volleyball and go skiing. A few days ago there was a funny incident: I climbed up on the window to close the transom. Suddenly Svetlov ran up to me, caught me around the waist, and lifted me down. Everybody gasped, and I was so embarrassed that I ran away. Afterward they all laughed at me and Svetlov. But, generally, Svetlov is disgusting; he is always trying to put his arms around you or something else of the kind. I received a letter from Nastya and still have not answered it. She asked me to send her a hat, but, to be frank, I have no patience to bother with hats.

February 21

Grigory Konstantinovich Ordzhonikidze is dead. Lida, Svetlana, Lena Gershman, and I went to the Hall of Columns at the House of Trade Unions.

Loss after loss: Kirov, Kuybyshev, Gorky, Ordzhonikidze—our old guard is dying off. . . .

Today Mulka, Vovka, and I went with the TETs* workers to Red Square. We saw all the leaders on the reviewing stand.

On February 7th we had a costume ball dedicated to Pushkin. I was dressed as Masha, the Captain's daughter, in a long orange dress with white lace around the throat and on the sleeves. And, of course, I wore a mask. I felt

* Central Thermo-Electric Power Station.

wonderful all evening. The costume was very good for dancing. Svetlana was the Queen of Shemakha, and Valya was a Circassian girl. My costume was judged the best.

Today I finally answered Nastya. I wrote her about the New Year's Eve parties, the skating rink, the hat, the skis, the Institute, Ordzhonikidze, and so on.

I received her letter February 1st, and only answered it today. So that's how things are!

March 4

A strange thing happened recently.

We have a new teacher in the Constitution class. Everybody likes him because he isn't like a teacher and explains everything very well. One day Svetlana and I saw him as we were coming from school. He was also on his way home, going in the same direction. We walked together.

Svetlana came to her corner and turned off, and we went on. We talked of this and that. He asked me whether we liked him. I said yes.

Yesterday I was walking home by myself, and suddenly I saw him again. When I passed him, he joined me. It was slippery, and he took me under the arm. Then he wrote down my telephone and asked whether I would go to the movies with him. I refused. And finally, to top it all, he asked me not to tell Svetlana, because she might babble.

I came home all flustered. What shall I do now? Let's

see what happens next. He is a Party member, middle-aged.

March 7

Oh, what shall I do? He doesn't leave me alone!

For two days I walked home with Svetlana. We took a different way, and, of course, I told her everything. She was very indignant.

And yesterday we took the old way and stopped for a while at Svetlana's corner. I thought I would not meet him again when I went on in my direction. I walked fast, with my eyes down. But he seemed to be waiting for me. He came over, said hello, and walked alongside. I said that I had just left Svetlana. He appeared frightened and asked, "Where?" Nevertheless, he walked me home. When we came to the house, I ran up the steps without offering him my hand and said, "Good-bye." And he said, "Good-day." I wanted to shout, "And you have a bad day!" Disgusting creature! This won't lead to any good. Even now I sit at his classes as though on needles, as though something hit me. How disgusting it all is!

March 21

Spring. The snow is melting, rivulets run down the street. It makes you want to run and jump, but the third quarter is just ending, and we have tests every day. Yesterday we had to write a composition on literature. My topic was "Why Belinsky called Pushkin's *Yevgeny Onegin* an encyclopedia of Russian life." I wrote three pages.

Vacation is coming soon. A short one, but I am glad, and so is everybody else. With the coming of spring, we have all gone a little mad. The effect of spring.

I bought myself a hat, inexpensive, but lovely. It will go beautifully with my red dress. I can't wait for May Day!

March 25

Something frightful and incomprehensible has happened: they arrested Uncle Misha, father's brother, and his wife, Anya. Irma, our little cousin, was sent to a children's home. They say that Uncle Misha was involved with some counterrevolutionary organization. What is going on? Uncle Misha, a member of the Party from the very first days of the Revolution—and suddenly an enemy of the people!

March 27

I can't understand what is happening to mother. All she does is scream and scold.

Today I scrubbed the floors, bought bread, went to the hospital for her, washed all the dishes, and took care of Verochka all day. Then I happened to touch Lelya's toys, Lel'ka began to squeal (her tears are never far), and mother swooped down on me like a hawk to defend her. I got smacked too. And she screamed at me—I'm nasty, I'll be an old maid, and so on, and so forth. All right, to the devil with her. Mother always takes Lel'ka's part.

March 29

I cried again today. It's all mother's fault. She scolds me all day. What does she want? Life has become a daily torture. . . . I wish I could go to father in the Far East. . .

April 16

My birthday passed unnoticed. Only Tonya gave me a present—a little red purse. Everybody has forgotten us and our mother.

And now another dreadful thing. It's beyond understanding. Stella's father was arrested. He was a department chief at the People's Commissariat of Heavy Industry. They say he was a wrecker. . . .

Yesterday I had a fight with the boys. One of the kids began to throw sand at Denisova, and she was scared and kept quiet. She hasn't got a bit of self-respect. The girls were playing volleyball, and the game broke up. I was just standing and waiting. Then I saw one of the boys bending down to pick up some sand to throw at me. But before he had a chance to raise his hand, I rushed at him and pulled at his collar so hard that his shirt tore, then hit him in the face. And . . . stopped! That was my mistake. I should have given him a thorough beating after I started, but I stopped. The kid took advantage of it and punched me in the nose and the eye. I saw sparks, and he, naturally, ran away. . . .

Now I laugh at it, but yesterday I was furious—most of all at myself. I ought to know how to fight properly.

April 17

Yesterday we had a Komsomol meeting. It lasted from eight in the evening until two in the morning. The subject on the agenda was "Criticism and Self-criticism." The director gave us a short report on Stalin's speech on this question. Then we began to offer criticism. The director got most of it. And for good reason. A stick-in-the-mud, not a director. I also spoke and attacked him. I said everything that had been on my mind for a long time—about the poor discipline, about our section leader, and about him personally. . . . It was a good speech. I got my share of criticism too: they said that I've stopped paying attention to my schoolwork, that I don't come to political study sessions, and so on. They are right. I really haven't been doing anything lately. . . .

I cannot stop thinking about my two little orphaned cousins. At least, Stella is still with her mother, but poor Irma has been put away into a children's home.

April 30

Hurrah, tomorrow, is May Day!

Yesterday we had a concert at school. We saw a play, *How Steel Was Tempered*. From school we went to the

Institute. They had a masked ball, and what magnificent costumes! I met Zhenechka and kissed her. She has grown very thin, but she looked striking in her Spanish costume.

May 3

Vacation is over. Instead of feeling rested after these three days, I am even more exhausted. May 1st I went to the demonstration. On the 2nd I went to Sokolniki on a May Day outing, and in the evening I ended up at the operetta theatre—saw *The Fair at Sorochinsk*.

Seven more days until exams!

May 21

Today we had dictation. Tomorrow, a written test on literature.

I'm bored to death, I long for something new, something I've never known. I mope from corner to corner all day and don't know what to do. I crochet, sew, embroider, anything but prepare for the exams. Maybe I ought to start a flirtation with somebody? What a pity that . . . No, I had better close the diary before I . . . oh, well. . . .

June 13

Exams are over. I was lucky almost until the end. Got "good" and "excellent." But flunked German—"poor." Drew the following conclusion: German is no joke;

without it I can't get into the Institute. Consequently, I must make a real effort and catch up with it!

June 20

The day before yesterday we came to the country. Everybody says I am looking better even after these two days. But I am still pursued by boredom. I cannot understand it—what is it I want? I remember Khvalynsk. Last year at this time I was on the Volga. . . . And Nastya doesn't write.

July 3

Time rolls along lazily. I embroider, read.

Today we went berry-picking. I love picking berries, but only alone. Today I deliberately went far, far away from the others. They hallooed and hallooed to me. I heard them, but kept silent. I like walking in the woods by myself, and I am never afraid, which seems to astonish everybody.

We're in a beautiful place. I found a little hollow, all green and full of flowers, with a brook running along it. The other day I went there and picked a lovely bouquet of daisies and cornflowers. A quiet, deserted spot, hardly anyone comes here.

We go to swim in the Moskva River. The path runs between two wooded hills. A morainal landscape, with many huge boulders along the road and in the water. The boulders make it bad for swimming here.

I have just read Stella's diary (it was a very dishonest action) and wondered at how advanced she is despite her twelve years. One of her adventures made me laugh. Apostol (a tough kid from the next village) was pestering her, but she wrote about it in her diary as if he were in love with her. Therefore she described the repulsive brat as very handsome and interesting.

July 6

Back in this little village. I went to Moscow for a day and, although I had many things to do, I had an excellent time.

I went to the movies and saw some Spaniards. There were about twelve of them, all of them in very original and striking dress. All of them extremely interesting and young. I looked at one especially. However, all the people in the theatre couldn't take their eyes from them.

The film, *A Little Mother*, was very good.

It's raining outside. It's been pouring for two days, and we can't go out anywhere. Today, Aunt Katya had a fight with the cleaning woman, and I got a scolding too. A lot was said in a few words. Papa is far away. He wouldn't have let us spend the summer with our high and mighty relatives!

July 13

Lovely days. Lovely mood. But something is lacking. I know what, but we shall say nothing, we shall say nothing of it. . . .

I am embroidering a pitcher with white and yellow daisies. Everybody says my embroidery is beautiful.

Yesterday we walked to Tuchkovo. We came back at night. There was crashing thunder, lightning flashed like broken arrows or flared over the whole dark cloudy sky. But though there was much noise, rain did not come. Everybody, especially Anya, my new friend, cried out and jumped with terror at every thunderburst, and huddled together like sheep. But I felt gay. The fiery flashes and the clattering thunder that followed made me wildly elated. I wanted to shout and sing.

July 28

A miserable summer. Frequent rains. Now, too, the sky is heavy with clouds. It will probably start raining soon.

Recently, I had a frightening experience. Stella and I went swimming. I stood on a rock, washing myself, and Stella stepped into a wasp nest. She ran aside, and the whole swarm of wasps flew out and attacked me. I ran to the middle of the field like a crazed horse, kicking and waving my arms, but this infuriated the wasps still more and they stung me without regard for their own lives. It was only after a while that I had sense enough to stand still. The wasps buzzed and circled around me for a few minutes, and then returned to their nest. However, I had gotten many stings—my whole body itches. The worst thing is that Stella, who was to blame for it all, got only one bite. . . . But I was angry only until

Stella began to describe how I kicked and rushed all over the clearing, how funny my eyes looked, full of fear and pain. She described it so vividly that we both laughed and laughed until our stomachs began to hurt.

August 11

After lunch yesterday we went to Tuchkovo to buy bread—Stella, Lelya, and I. We bought the bread and went to the station. Lelya and I walked over to look at the locomotive. A man with a blackened face and shiny eyes and teeth, probably a machinist or stoker, asked what we were looking at. We began to ask him questions, and he very willingly told us all about the locomotive. We liked him very much and gave him an apple when we were saying good-bye. Lelya had even decided that she would become a machinist when she grew up, but he advised her to take up flying.

I have made great advances this summer with my guitar. I have learned several waltzes, foxtrots, and songs. The summer is ending, there are only a few days left before school. I hope they pass quickly, I miss school. . . .

Nastya does not write. I feel sad and hurt.

August 22

A dreadful misfortune has hit our landlords.

Today our landlord unexpectedly came home from work at noon. Marusya, his daughter, thought he was sick, he was so upset and pale. But two other men came in after him and began to search the house. They went through the landlord's rooms, then started on ours. These people were full of an odd icy courtesy. I was so stunned, I could not move. The landlord's linen closet stood in our room. After they looked through the closet, the two NKVD agents wanted to search our things too, but the landlord told them that we were summer visitors. He was chalk white and so confused that when they pointed at me and asked, "Is this your daughter?" he said, "Yes!" Afterward they all went to the landlord's part of the house and talked about something for a long time. Then we heard the landlord saying loudly, with a break in his voice, as if keeping back his tears, "Well, good-bye. . . ." Then everybody burst out crying and, loudest of all, Marusya. She rushed to her father screaming, "Daddy, daddy . . . Where are they taking you? . . ." The landlord could no longer restrain himself and started crying. Marusya clung to him so desperately that I began to cry too. He finally tore himself away from her and quickly walked out. The two polite, cold men walked out after him.

They went. And everybody, including us, cried. I went to the landlord's rooms and tried to console Marusya. When she calmed down a little, she suddenly jumped up:

"I'm going after him!"

After lunch Marusya came back with her mother. As soon as her mother entered, she began to wail. Grandmother tried to console her, and the landlady said that her husband had been arrested on suspicion of Trotskyism.

I thought about it for a long time. I remembered the arrests of Irma's and Stella's fathers. Something strange is happening. I thought and thought, and came to the conclusion: if my father also turns out to be a Trotskyite and an enemy of his country, I shall not be sorry for him!

I wrote this, but (I confess) there is a gnawing worm of doubt. . . .

August 29

The three of us—Stella, Lelya, and I—are sitting in comfortable chairs near the lake in the park. The girls are eating ice cream. Little steamboats are moving on the lake, filled with people like baskets full of flowers. And here is another interesting sight: the sound of a shot, and a multicolored little cloud appears in the sky, floating rapidly.

It is pleasant to relax in the park. Beautiful fountains, picturesque arbors, pools.

We have been in Moscow since August 25th, but I have not done anything I had planned. I haven't even been to school. I met Lida. She is in trouble—she wasn't promoted because she failed in physics.

Yesterday I went to see Lena Gershman. She had just returned from Sochi, where she had a lovely time. She was delighted to see me, and we decided to sit together at school again.

September 10

A few days ago I went to see Vanya, our Komsomol

organizer. He had invited me to talk about Laura. Her father and mother were arrested; Laura herself is eighteen, no longer a minor. He wanted to know what I thought of her. Laura is practically out in the street now: for the time being, she is staying with a girl friend, but the girl's parents will soon return from the country, and Laura will have no place to live. A frightful situation. Vanya insisted that she must be expelled from the Komsomol. I disagreed, but he kept insisting and arguing that she could not remain a member: she refused to repudiate her parents—enemies of the people. I finally agreed with the Komsomol organizer, but with the feeling that I was doing something bad. . . .

After this conversation, we had some disturbing events at home. Uncle Ilya, mother's brother, is working in the Transbaikal region, at the tin mines. A few days ago we sent him a telegram, but received a strange answer: "Undelivered. Addressee no longer here." We are all puzzled —where could he have gone? His wife Marina sent four more telegrams, but there is no answer. Everyone is in a terrible mood. Grandmother is crying. I cry. Where has Ilya disappeared to? And what if they should arrest my father too? No, no, I have faith in my father! He is a Party member, an old Civil War partisan, he never was and never will be an enemy of the people.

How black, how dreadful everything is!

My work in the Komsomol is interesting. I was assigned to work with the fifth year—Lelya's class. And I may be elected group organizer for my class. We have three Komsomol members—Nonna, Sergeyev, and I.

September 11

Another strange surprise: a telegram from father. He may return this fall. What can it mean? He went for two years, and suddenly he is coming back. I bawled, grandmother too. But mother only snorts, grumbles, and scolds: "What are you bawling about?" she keeps saying. "It's nonsense, there's no reason to cry." Nonsense! And what if they arrest father? . . . Our whole life will turn topsy-turvy.

But I will never repudiate my father!

September 13

We had a terribly upsetting meeting today. We took up Laura's case. She was expelled. All through the meeting she sat in the back row, behind everybody, and cried. Everyone was very depressed.

Sergeyev was elected group organizer for our class.

DEAR PAPA!
How are you out there? Lelya and I miss you very much. I am doing well at school and taking part in all the activities. I work with the Pioneers in Lelya's class. She is also good at school. Her eczema persists despite all treatment. I was elected to the Komsomol committee. Recently we took up the case of one of the girls. Her mother and father had been arrested. At first I disagreed with the motion to expel her, but later, the others convinced me, and I voted for the expulsion. Still, I am not certain that she should have been expelled. The girl cried, she did not want to leave the Komsomol, but at the

same time she said that she loved her mother and father and would never repudiate them. After the meeting, I felt terrible, and when I came home I cried for a long time. How is it her fault if her parents were arrested for something?

Come back soon, papa, if you can. It is dreary and lonely at home without you.

Many, many kisses,

Your loving daughter,
NINA

October 15

Lena Gershman is planning to leave school. She wants to give a farewell party at my house. But I am opposed to it. I'll be left without my best friend. We have an interesting relationship: we sit together, fool around together, but don't consider ourselves friends. This is what she told me yesterday when I said that I'll be left alone, without a friend. She seems to have forgotten everything: how I visited her when she was sick, our long walks, and that I confide all my thoughts and secrets to her. I was very hurt by her words yesterday. In the future I'll know better: I shall never open all of myself before a girl friend. . . . And yet, in spite of everything, I consider her my friend.

November 8

We had a cross-country race today, and I surprised everyone by my brilliant record. In the beginning I fell back and was one of the last, but in the middle of the race I added speed, overtook about ten runners, and came in third. For our school, I was first. Lena came to root for me and took such tender care of me that she even helped me put on my shoes. Our boys were represented by Zunka. He came in fifth. I looked after him, and he looked after me. I gave him a scarf (the poor kid was frozen stiff), and treated him to some candy, and he just followed me around and stared adoringly into my eyes.

November 23

What a busy, what a jolly, time! For the first time in my life I feel constantly drawn to school, I have no patience at all to stay home.

For a while after vacation, Lena Gershman and I began to feel bored in school: it seemed that there was suddenly nothing to do there. We did not have to run to classes, shout, argue, get excited. Lena and I have the same character. When there are things to be done, when we are up to our necks in work, rushing around busily, we are happy and gay. But the moment there is peace and quiet, and nothing to be done, a pall of depression seems to descend on us, and we begin to quarrel.

For the past ten days I've been meeting with my Pioneer squad every day. I have to organize a meeting devoted to the elections to the Supreme Soviet. When I came to class after the holidays, my kids seemed upset and did not want to remain after school and work. After long attempts to discover what was wrong, I finally got them to tell me: Antonov and Butenko have been demoralizing the whole class. They've been shooting holes in the wall newspaper with rubber bands. I managed to get the fourth unit together and convinced them to start work. Everything went well, and the kids decided to make a scale model of an election booth and publish a wall newspaper. The third unit has already built a marvelous model of a frontier post. And now they are preparing an album about Khrushchev, and other projects. My kids are doing many good things.

In connection with the Supreme Soviet elections, our school will be attached to the Writers' Union for agitation among the people. The writer Vsevolod Vishnevsky came to us and gave a talk. Yesterday we were divided into brigades, and the director himself appointed the brigadiers.

All the Komsomol members, even Nonka, were made brigadiers, except me. I am just a member of Shcherbakov's brigade. Many people wondered why I, a member of the Komsomol, was not a brigadier. I felt bad, but I realized that the director was merely taking petty revenge for my criticism at the Komsomol meeting. And, of course, I have no intention to complain to anyone. Nevertheless, Lena went to the director and protested indignantly that she, who was not in the Komsomol, had been appointed brigadier, while Kosterina, a Komsomol activist, was only a rank-and-file participant. I don't know what was said there, but, as Lena told me afterward, the director said that this was not to be regarded as an expression of his distrust or lack of confidence in me.

After the list of brigadiers was announced to us, we went to our teacher in charge, Tatyana Alexandrovna. She also noticed that I had been wronged. I told her about my clashes with the director last year. She convinced me that my honor as a Komsomol member demanded that I should rise above such trifles and prove my social maturity by my work. Tatyana Alexandrovna really reassured me and inspired me with so much confidence that I made a decision: the brigade will work, in fact, under my leadership.

November 24

Well, our work is going full blast. Yesterday we went canvassing the homes assigned to our brigade. We were to meet the writer Fishberg. We visited many apartments and talked to the tenants, telling them where the election committee was, advising them for whom to vote, and so on. But we never found the "activist" Fishberg.

November 30

The day before yesterday was very foggy. The fog lasted all day and all night and all day yesterday until evening. Lena and I ran through the streets, observing the life of the city in the fog. The whole city, so familiar since childhood, all the streets and squares and alleys were changed as in a fairy tale. All the sharp, angular lines became blurred, the buildings seemed taller and wider. Even the sounds were drowned and muted. We walked, listened, and looked. It was very interesting: even the sidewalk across the street was invisible! Cars moved slowly with their headlights on and blew their horns continually. Streetcars and buses inched along cautiously, their bells ringing. And yet there were many accidents. Pedestrians looked like shadows two or three steps away, and then melted into the fog.

Yesterday, Lena, Grisha Grinblat, and I came to Tatyana Alexandrovna's to work. We are preparing an exhibition for the Twentieth Anniversary of the Revolution. The members of the history circle are taking an active part in it. I worked with enthusiasm—writing, cutting out, pasting. Tatyana Alexandrovna was very pleased with my work. But I also found time to flirt with Grisha. Tatyana Alexandrovna said I had a crush on him. Of course that's nonsense. After we finished, Tatyana Alexandrovna served us tea, and I acted as hostess at the table. She is a remarkable person, and I wonder why she is not a Party member.

December 2

Life at school is full and interesting. As soon as classes are over, there is rushing and noise everywhere: here there is a Pioneer assembly, with the sounds of bugles and rapid drumbeats; there someone runs past with a banner; in the classrooms the circles are in session—dramatic, musical, choral, and so on. My fifth-year kids are making decorations.

The director has loosened his purse strings and allotted some money for breakfast for the Komsomol activists. We devour the rolls with salami like starved, greedy wolf cubs.

Yesterday I worked till I was ready to drop. I was preparing the material on peasant rebellions, then the revolutions of 1905 and 1917. When we finished, Lena and I remained to wait for Tatyana Alexandrovna. Lena and I are becoming closer and closer friends. And we both love Tatyana Alexandrovna. Yesterday we had a good laugh when that gossip Aronova said that Tatyana Alexandrovna was supposedly flirting with the boys!

This Aronova is a model of stupidity and . . . just generally a windbag!

Oh, well, let me get to my homework.

December 13

Preparations for the elections and election day were full of excitement. Our brigade issued two wall newspapers and canvassed many homes. On election day I was up at half-past five in the morning. I put on my best dress and ran to school, although watch duty did not start till noon. At school, I monitored till nine. By ten I was with my Pioneers. And at twelve I went on watch duty again until three in the afternoon. The school was decorated beautifully: rugs, curtains, pictures, posters. That day I had my fill of taxi rides. I visited old women and sick people, took them to the polling place, and then back home. Vsevolod Vishnevsky* stood at the table be-

* A Soviet writer.

fore the urns and greeted everyone with a few pleasant words. Several times I went into the booths myself, helping the illiterate.

This day will remain in my memory for a long time. The writer Fishberg, evidently moved by the general holiday mood, began to shower me with attentions. The silly fool! To myself, I call him a mattress: pudgy, baggy, with glasses on his nose. Keeps begging me to teach him to skate.

December 15

I received a letter from father:

Dear Nina!

Forgive me for not writing you. I am not in a letter-writing mood, and I'll tell you why. I was expelled from the Party and, consequently, dismissed from my post. I shall not go into details: at your age much will still be unclear to you. But you must remember one thing: you will need a great deal of calm and endurance now. I do not know as yet how events will turn for me. But even in the worst case, you must be sure that your father was never a scoundrel or double-dealer, and has never blemished his name by anything dirty or base. And therefore—be steadfast! Of course, these are difficult days, but we must not and should not lose courage. We shall live through and overcome all ordeals. Believe me that your dad still has "enough powder in his powder keg," and has no intention to bow before adversity.

Regards to Lelya and Verushka. Kiss mama and grandmother and all the rest.

Your dad

I wanted to cry out, "I hear you, dad!" I am afraid that we must be prepared for some very bad developments.

December 19

The writer Fishberg is beginning to annoy me. After the concert at the Writers' House, where we heard such remarkable performers as Borisov, Rina Zelenaya, Khenkin, and others, Fishberg began to telephone me all the time, although he seldom found me home. Mama did not like it. I told her to send him packing. She did, but he continued to call. Then I asked him myself to stop those calls. Honestly, I've been disgusted with him ever since the concert. A lovely evening was spoiled by all those handclasps and compliments and . . . Generally, all of it is very repulsive. I told Lena about it and, incidentally, expressed my opinion about such men. "It seems to me," I said, "that a man who runs after young girls is a vile creature! Naturally, I immediately begin to hate such men and send them to the devil!"

But Lena argued that we are grown-up girls now and begin to attract attention. Nevertheless, I think I was right.

December 20

There was a terrible and ugly row at home today.

A friend of papa's, Esfir Pavlovna, just came from the Far East and telephoned us. Mama was out, and I spoke to her. She asked how we were. She knows a great deal about our life: she is a party member, and papa told her everything. I said that Uncle Misha and Aunt Anya had been arrested and we had no news of them, and that Irma, my cousin, was in an orphanage. I also said that I heard that Uncle Vasya, papa's brother, was expelled from the Party. He is supposed to have said that he liked Lenin more than Stalin. Esfir Pavlovna said that papa is managing to keep in good spirits and is not losing courage. Although he is not working, he still receives his salary. His case will be examined by Moscow.

When I finished the conversation, grandmother pounced on me for telling everything to strangers. I said that Esfir Pavlovna knows father and his affairs, and, besides, I shall not conceal anything, and will tell everything in school too. She shouted that I must not do anything of the kind, and that none of it concerns me anyway. When I repeated that I would not lie or conceal things, she rushed at me, threw me on the bed and began to choke me, screaming, "I'll murder you!" I also flew into a rage. I broke away from her and screamed that she was an old witch, and that she was unworthy of the pension she was getting because her husband, an old Bolshevik, had been killed in the Civil War. . . .

They are obviously afraid—my aunts and grandmother. . . . And I fell into despair after this dreadful fight. . . .

Papa, darling papa, I cannot wait to see you home. . . .

[1938]

January 10

The holidays are over. New Year's Eve was gay. Just before New Year's we had good news: we finally heard from Ilya. He sent us a telegram, for some reason from Chita instead of Khapcheranga. And papa sent us money.

Another friend of papa's—Andryusha—came to Moscow from the Far East. He is young and jolly, and a little mischievous. He told us a lot about the Far East and about papa. The question of his Party membership has not yet been decided. He is accused of contacts with his brothers and with many of those who have now been declared enemies of the people—Bukharin, Radek, and others. Before the Revolution, papa knew many people in the revolutionary movement, and now he is blamed for it. What am I, a total fool, not to understand this?

Andryusha stayed with us a whole week and spent his money right and left. He gave us all chocolates, bought cakes, and took us to the theatre.

At school we also had a party. Two accordions, a band, a buffet, and dancing. We had guests—the young people from TETs. I came home at four in the morning.

Lena was hysterical all evening and flirted wildly with the boys, but I saw that she was on the verge of tears. She has had difficulties with her schoolwork lately and had to work hard to pull up her marks for the last quarter.

I danced with the Pioneer leader Valya, and even out-did myself in some folk dancing.

Today I received a letter from Irma in the children's home. She is very lonely and cries a great deal. She wants to get out of the home. If papa were here, we would take her to live with us. . . . But mother and grandmother?

I spoke to Tatyana Alexandrovna about Irma. Tatyana Alexandrovna feels very sorry for her and gave me some money for her. People like Tatyana Alexandrovna are very rare and must be appreciated and treasured! Poor woman, she looks very bad now and is practically sick over Vitka Novoselov. He is being kicked out of school for rowdyism. She vouched for him twice, and now she feels terribly hurt. But something seems to have happened to her personally, too, although she keeps it from us. She warned us recently to cut down our contacts with her, or we would get into difficulties with the director. As for the director, I had a big fight with him over the wall newspaper. In fact, we had such a heated "argument" that he threw me out of his office. But no one will ever make me turn away from Tatyana Alexandrovna, no matter what happens.

January 11

Lena came to see me today. Things are very bad for her at home: her father gave her a beating, her mother is also against her, and both of them keep nagging and scolding her. Her father mentioned me in abusive terms. He insinuated that we keep some sort of "bad company" and generally "hang around" heaven knows where. Her mother is even planning to speak to mine. I tried to calm her down: all girls of our age are suspected of something or other and watched. I had less of it, she had more.

A few minutes after she left, her mother telephoned to ask where she was. They certainly keep her under surveillance!

January 14

Had a fight with Lena in class. I called her a fool for some silly reason. This expression is very frequent in our conversations. Lenka slapped me on the face with a copybook, and I angrily called her an idiot. . . . However, we quickly made up.

I must confess, though, that I have a rotten character. I cannot stand rudeness or being screamed at. As soon as anything of the kind happens, I flare up and turn into a beast.

February 27

Yesterday Lena received her Komsomol card. I recommended her about a month ago. Now we have seven Komsomol members in our class. Lena has already put on her pin and walks around beaming. And after the first Komsomol meeting, she ran up and kissed me. The kids started laughing, and Lena burst out crying . . . with happiness! I remember how excited and happy I was when I first joined the Komsomol organization. Now I feel much calmer and more confident.

April 1

The holidays were quite pleasant. I was at the Hall of Columns. On March 30th I went to Maly Theatre to see *The Forest*. Two evenings I went walking with Grisha Grinblat. We walked to the center of the city, to Red Square. Lida was with us. After we walked her home, Grisha walked back with me. We exchanged a lazy word now and then—everything had already been "talked out." Suddenly, when we were already near my house, he asks: "What about that fellow, whatever his name . . . the 'Constitution' fellow . . . did he telephone you?" I just stared at him. In a moment of frankness I had told him one day how "Constitution" had tried to court me. But I felt offended when he brought up that almost forgotten incident, and we parted coldly. Generally, I must put a stop to these walks. I don't want to spoil my relations with Lena. Our friendship has been badly shaken lately. It is not the old untroubled friendship; there are little spots of misunderstanding here and there. I think that Grisha is very important to her, although she would not admit it. Compared to the other boys, Grisha is pretty eccentric, but he is more innocent than the rest. However, the devil knows them. . . .

Life at school flows along its usual course, and one day is like another. There are still six weeks before exams.

Soon it will be summer. Will we go anywhere? I'd love to go to Khvalynsk. . . .

Yesterday I was in a miserable mood. Black, heavy thoughts whirled through my mind, but there was no rainstorm (tears). And that's probably bad, because after crying comes sleep, and, this way, I stayed awake till three in the morning.

April 12

Yesterday we received a telegram: "Sent you two thousand. Don't expect any more. Coming June." We did not understand a thing. His work term is not over, and yet papa is coming home. There must be more complications. . . .

Yesterday we celebrated my seventeenth birthday. I did not want any celebration, but mama and grandmother insisted. Now grandmother is ill after too much drinking last night. My guests were Lena, Lida, and Laura. The table was by no means empty, and we even drank wine, but the party was not much fun. Lelya alone made everybody laugh after a couple of drinks and saved us from boredom.

April 13

The writer Fishberg suddenly called me again. Asked why I forgot him and didn't telephone. I didn't know what to say. Then he asked me to call him whenever it would be convenient for me. Like an idiot, I became confused and said I would. Of course, I will not call him. He disgusts me, especially since my visit to his apartment. This is what happened:

For the first time since I began this diary, I'll speak about my appearance. I know I am not pretty, and my dear relatives remind me of it quite often. Sometimes I feel terrible about it. There are times when I think that nobody can ever love me.

So when this roly-poly began to stare at me and call me and assure me that he liked me, I became confused like a fool and began to answer him, although he is a nasty, flabby little man, real trash. One day, before going on vacation, he telephoned and said that he was very anxious to see me, would I come up. And I went. I didn't want to, yet I went, as if pulled by a leash. I came, took off my coat, and sat down on the sofa—a vile, shabby, creaky sofa. It smelled of dust and mold and bedbugs. He sat down near me and began to read Mayakovsky's poems, and his own. He read badly, in a silly singsong. I felt nauseated. And he, who considers himself a poet, didn't have the slightest idea of what was happening inside me. This jellyfish tried to embrace and kiss me. I pushed him away violently, with all my strength (and I seem to have inherited my father's strength), put on my coat, and left. He mumbled something and fussed around me. . . . And now he called again, and I didn't have enough character to answer him as he deserves!

Today I visited Tatyana Alexandrovna—she is sick. Lena came too. She spoke about the situation with her family. She is really in a bad way. Her father is twice as old as her mother, a dreadful egotist and petty, too. For instance, he "allots" his wife money for household expenses in driblets. Such piggishness! My father brings his pay home, turns out his pockets, and says to mother: "Here, mother, take it and do your planning!"

Lena told us many outrageous details. And when we went home, she spoke about herself. She said she had no willpower at all, and that she didn't care whether she lived or died. She almost talked herself into confession and justification of suicide. I was frightened and said that I had gloomy and depressed moods too. Lena said that everything else was nonsense, but she had a truly great sorrow. I asked whether it had to do with her family. "No." "Grisha?" She said, "Yes." And told me frankly that she loves him. . . .

I recalled my walks with Grisha and reread what I had written on April 1st. Such foolishness! I wanted to cross it out, but changed my mind: if I cross out all the foolish things, I'll have to cross out half the diary.

April 15

Well! I have just heard a declaration of love! And from whom? Heavens, even the diary will be surprised and burst out laughing! Grisha! I don't want to and I cannot write about it now. I don't know how I got home after he told me. I cannot eat, I cry and I laugh. Lelya looks at me with alarm. I don't know what to do, and try to stuff her with candy. She is surprised and refuses

to take it. I tell her that I got "excellent" in school.
She does not believe me. . . .

April 17

I've calmed down a little, and now I can write down
what happened.

When Lena told me she had a great sorrow, I decided
to find out from Grisha how he felt about Lena. He was
walking me home and I asked whether he had any sorrows. He said he didn't. Then I asked, was he suffering
about anything? And he said, "One doesn't speak about
such things." I persisted, and asked how he felt about
Lena. He said frankly that he had stopped noticing her
and had cooled off toward her. "Why?" I insisted, since
I considered him a friend, and nothing else. Then he
said, "I like you, Ninka, I like you very much." I tried
to turn it into a joke and said that he was still a kid, that
Lena was a fine girl, and a pretty one, and that I could
not imagine how he could possibly fall in love with me
after Lena.

"You think Lena is pretty?" he asked. I said yes, and
was completely sincere. Lena is really a very pretty girl.
"And I would not like you to be like her!" said Grisha.

We walked for a long time after that, and I said to
him in parting: "You may feel whatever you wish about
me, but I still consider you only a friend." He held my
hand in his and asked me to forgive him for blurting out
his secret. "You insisted on it yourself." "Nonsense," I

said, "don't get upset about it. How cold your hands are. . . . Good-bye, Grisha."

But when I entered the gateway, my legs turned to water and I pressed myself to the wall. . . .

Yesterday our meeting was a little strained. He was embarrassed and upset, and there was a guilty look in his eyes. Today he was calmer.

Lena is in a dreadful state. She does not do her assignments and sits at the desk, dull and apathetic. I feel very sorry for her, but I don't know how to help her. I am not in love with Grisha, there's simply a good, comradely feeling. . . . But then, who knows . . . If this goes on, I may even fall in love.

April 20

I had a strange dream last night.

Grisha and I were sitting at a table in some room, so near that our heads touched. Lena was also in the room doing something behind us. She asked, "What are you talking about?" We turned our faces to one another and smiled, without answering Lena. A strand of my hair fell over my forehead, and I wanted to put it back, but our heads were so close that my hand brushed against Grisha's hair, and I stroked it. It was very pleasant to touch his hair. Then Lena said, "Well, I'm going." And we went to walk her home. She seemed to be going to give birth to her second child. I wondered, "But where is the first?" But she did not answer. Somebody screamed, but Grisha said, "It's nothing to be alarmed about," and I calmed down. . . .

What silly nonsense one dreams of!

The radio was just playing Tchaikovsky's romance, "I do not know whether I love you, but it seems to me that I do." I've become amazingly romantic lately, I've even begun to love the moon. . . . Last night I looked for it, but did not find it.

April 22

Last evening Grisha and I agreed by telephone to meet earlier today, to go to the museum. As we were walking, we bumped into Nina and Olga. They began to giggle and make hints about us, about our being inseparable, always together. We hurried away from them. I was so embarrassed that I could not say anything for a long time. When we came to the museum, we met a group of kids, Lena among them. It seemed to me that she gave me a probing look. Well, it's time for her to guess at the truth. After our visit to the museum, Lena went home at once, although I begged her to come up to my house.

I've lost a lot of weight these past few days, and everybody at home keeps asking why I've become so thin, am I in love?

Incidentally, Grisha confessed recently that he has begun to keep a diary again. I wonder if he'll ever let me read it.

April 23

Every day I become more and more convinced that

the girl whom Grisha will love will be a lucky girl. Grisha's love ennobles a person.

Yesterday he was absent from school. I wanted to telephone him. I walked back and forth past the office door, but could not bring myself to go in. When I came home, they told me that some boy had called. I guessed that it was Grisha and waited all evening for a second call. It never came. This morning I called him myself.
. . .

There was a thin, unpleasant drizzle. All pedestrians hurried by close to the walls and gateways, but Grisha and I walked and walked over the Moscow streets. We did not want to be with other people, we preferred to get wet and feel only each other's presence. And we talked and talked. Then suddenly he asked, "May I take you by the arm?" I said, "Of course." He had thought about it all evening, and did not dare to ask.

Today I went to his house to do the algebra lessons. After algebra Grisha began to read me his poems, and the moment I'd say I liked a poem, he'd tear it out of the copybook and give it to me.

Late Autumn

Late autumn. Everything is gray and dull,
The wind spits blasts of leaves.
The cold has shackled everything alive.
Sad, gray, and gloomy is the sky.

> Time races. Only a short while ago
> The air caressed us, drunk without wine.
> Time, people, everything was drunk,
> Everything sang "It's spring."

Late autumn. But the glints of May
Live in my heart despite the dark.
I walked you home. . . . That tender day,
How long ago!

> Late autumn. Wilted, sere
> The leaves of lilacs and of roses.
> People have grown more sober and severe.
> Late autumn. Frost.

I like the last verse best. The others aren't bad, either. But this is a poem Grisha wrote, not under my influence, but "someone else's" and . . . his first dedication was not to me. This hurts me bitterly. Above the poem, he wrote, "To Nina."

At the height of our poetic evening, Grisha's mother came in. I was embarrassed, but she was very pleasant to me. When he walked me home, we spoke about the future. He wants to become a scientist, and I am trying to dissuade him. He said that a scientist must dedicate himself wholly to science, and therefore he would never marry. I answered (and it came out so simply!): "But, of course, that can never be, you can see it yourself!" He was embarrassed and fell silent.

May 2

On April 30th Grisha and I went to see the gala illumination. We walked to the center of the city, along the embankment, but there was nothing new. Our conversation was more interesting than the lights. We spoke of many things. Later, when we were already on the

way home, I said that I would transfer to another school
next year. "Why?" "Well, perhaps I won't, depending
on circumstances." He interpreted this as meaning that
I was tired of him, and said quietly:

> "I'm melting the windowpane with my brow.
> Will there or won't there be love?
> And will it be great, or will it be tiny?"

"The latter seems more likely, I guess," he concluded.
My lips trembled, and my eyes filled with tears. It
hurt me to think that he considered our love "tiny." I
felt sad that all of this would soon be over. He noticed
my tears and became upset, trying to find out what was
wrong with me. I explained to him why I wanted to
transfer to another school. "It will be painful for me to
remain in this school if everything ends between us."
He had thought that I was seeing him just "for lack of
something better to do," that I was simply amusing myself with him. I was shocked, and told him in veiled
words that I love him. He glowed with joy and begged
forgiveness for his words. We parted reconciled and
promised each other to avoid misunderstandings in the
future.

And yesterday was May 1st, and I woke at six in the
morning in an excellent mood. I came to school before
anyone else. But when two cars came from TETs, all the
kids came running. We piled in noisily and drove off to
TETs. There we started a game of volleyball. We
played with great excitement, but Grisha is a poor player
and I felt annoyed watching him. Two hours later, our

columns came marching and I saw Lena. I was very happy she had come. We both had a marvelous time and felt wonderful. It started raining, but this made us even happier. Zunka had no jacket, and I offered him a corner of my coat. He put his arm around my shoulders and we covered ourselves by the coat. Grisha walked ahead, gloomy and scowling. He irritated me. Why wasn't he having fun, why couldn't he have put his arm around my shoulders, like Zunka? I ran and jumped and sang and even danced. This was after the march on Red Square. We walked in a jolly company and came on a group of soldiers, dancing the lesginka. One was pushed out into the center of the circle. I cried out, "Come on, come on!" Somebody pushed me forward, and I joined him in the dance. I danced like a wild one. The soldiers and all our kids applauded. They all congratulated me, "Atta-boy, Ninka!"

And Grisha did not come with us; he took the placards back to the car.

I came home with numb feet. I went to bed, but sleep wouldn't come. I kept thinking about Grisha and reviewing everything that had happened that day. And I kept asking myself: "Do I love him, or don't I?" And came to a decision. But I won't say it now, I don't want to draw conclusions yet.

Today several of us, including Grisha, went to the stadium to see a football game. Grisha had given me his diary before the holidays, and I read it straight through. I liked only the beginning, where he criticized me for speaking up against him. After that came comments on

Turgenev, then a discussion of our relations. I did not like the diary. Everything but the beginning seemed written to order. There is little sincerity, much is left unsaid. For example, there is nothing about Lena, although there should have been a lot. I had the feeling that Grisha had been writing the diary for me. There ıs not much about our relations, but he writes directly: "I love her very much, and I think that if I see her in ten years, and she is married, I will go on loving her tenderly and strongly anyway." And "I love Nina very much, so much that it simply amazes me that I (he wrote "a man" at first, then crossed it out) could be capable of such a strong feeling. Perhaps we shall be closer to each other in the future, perhaps we shall become related. Will I be happy? Completely. Not because I will possess her, but because I shall be able to be with her a long time, I shall be able to talk and talk with her, to anticipate her slightest wish, to get my fill of looking at her darling face. Will this time ever come? Come, come, I long for you." He lavishes endearments on me, calls me "Ninoch-ka." He is a good boy. But just a boy, nothing more. He still believes you can keep loving for ten years!

May 3

Lida has just been to see me. She spoke about her af-fairs, but most of all about boys. She says that as soon as she hears a declaration of love, the man becomes re-pulsive to her. Strange. If you love him, how can you feel like that?

But after the talk with Lida, I began to see more clearly what I had thought about before, but was afraid to admit to myself: I don't love Grisha. I write this calmly and confidently. I like Grisha, he is a very fine person, but I don't love him. It makes me very, very sad. And now it seems to me that I shall never love anyone, that I shall never be able to love anyone.

Poor boy! After all that has happened, after all that I said to him—and now . . . How can I tell him? I feel that I will not have the strength to tell him the truth. Perhaps I shall begin to love him in the future? But hardly! And Grisha says that he does not think he'll ever stop loving me. Do I love him, or don't I?

Shall I tell Lena? I've thought about it for a long time, and I've decided that I must. I shall give her my diary, let her read it. I hope she will understand me. . . . No, I won't give it to her! What if she interprets it altogether differently?

May 6

We had a gala evening at school last night. The students presented a play. I walked home with Petya. He read me a poem which he dedicated to me. He said he wrote it in a "fit of jealousy":

> Happiness flashed by—a soaring gull,
> Caught fire and scorched my soul,
> Then flitted on, alighted on a nearby dune,
> And burst into a bright and merry tune.

Naturally I told him I liked it, otherwise he would have torn it up. But I don't like it—he's straining for rhyme, but there is little sense. But what can you do with poets? Petya went on talking, telling me something, but I can't for the life of me remember what he said.

May 7

I gave Lena my diary. She read it and said, "I expected it from him, but not from you."

We took a long walk in the evening. It was raining, but we had an umbrella and we walked disregarding weather and time. At first Lena said, "After this, I do not love him any more." But then she repeated again and again that she loves him to the point of madness. For a long time I tried to console her and to assure her that the situation could be mended. She complained of her lack of character and envied mine (found something to envy, really!). Lena confessed that when she was with Grisha, she suddenly became tongue-tied and could not say anything. She also said she was jealous, and that it would be hard for all of us to be at the same school.

Today the three of us remained after classes to arrange certain materials. Lena was in a wretched mood. Grisha asked her why the funereal face. "It's nothing at all." She did not walk home with us.

I must admit that when we three are together, I find it doubly difficult: first, because I feel guilty, and second . . . because I am jealous! What a character. I am no longer sure that Grisha feels indifferent toward Lena.

But why should I care? After all, I don't love him. That's the whole trouble—I no longer understand myself. Now it seems to me that I do love him. He was so extraordinary today. He took a red ribbon I used as a bookmark from my book and would not give it back. I deliberately frowned and demanded it back. He also scowled and returned it. But how handsome he was at the moment!

Yesterday Lena assured me that I would come to love him, that he was a wonderful person and we were very well suited. She almost cried, called herself an idiot, and accused no one but herself for his cooling off. She had always been silent with him, he was bored, and the flame went out. . . .

May 10

Yesterday Grisha and I went walking, and suddenly he began to insist, "Tell me, tell me what you feel." I said, "I don't understand myself any more. I don't know whether I love you or not." He said that he wanted to be alone, and we said good-bye. In parting, he asked me not to think about it and to leave everything to time.

I feel rotten. All I long for is to get through with the exams and get away, as far as possible.

May 11

Dismal mood. I want to cry.

It's a strange thing. When I see him, it seems to me

that I don't love him. And when he's away, I go mad
with longing for him. . . .

Mama scolds. Uncle Misha came yesterday from Baku.
He had a few drinks with grandmother, and today he
went out somewhere and disappeared. Grandmother
went to the militia to report a missing person. She came
back even angrier, now she just sits there and drinks.

May 12

Yesterday Lena and I read Grisha's diary. He gave up
the first and began a new one on May 3rd, when he was
jealous of Petya and learned that I did not love him.

We went on an outing. The fellows had a volleyball
and two bicycles. I learned a little how to ride a bicycle.
Lena did not come. Grisha went around angry and
scowling. Yesterday Lena told me she was no longer
angry with me; it made her feel better that I didn't love
Grisha. Naturally; in his diary he wrote that he would
be more attentive to Lena. And I wrote in his diary:

> I wanted to write you, Grisha, but I spoiled a lot
> of paper and gave up. I cannot express what I would
> like to explain. Perhaps because there is a muddle in
> my head, and I cannot see anything clearly. But I
> want to say that you misunderstood me. You exag-
> gerate everything and draw absurd conclusions.
> Please don't rack your brains and don't ask me
> what this means. One day everything will be clear,
> but for the present let things go as they will. Time
> will show. I liked your diary. It is a good diary, and
> you yourself are very good, Grisha; you grow not

by the day, but by the hour, which makes me very happy.

N<small>INA</small>

May 14

Why am I suffering? I don't love him. Why, then, am I jealous of Lena? What a torture to see him turn away from me! During recess he walks with Lena. I pretend that I don't care what they are talking about. I am so angry and so lonely! Lena was gay all day today, and I was gloomy. He asked me, "What are you so angry at?" If he knew how much he hurt me with his words. Tomorrow we are going to the museum, but he did not say anything to me.

I just came home and telephoned him. He came running like a madman, could not catch his breath. We went walking. He asked whether I agreed to Lena's suggestion that we all go to the park and read each other's diaries. I flatly refused.

In school I was in a horrible mood, but now, when we were walking and talking together, we both felt happy. He repeated several times, "No new developments on our front."

May 16

We had a quarrel.

At school he suggested that I see Lena to the bus. I understood him and agreed. When Lena had left, he came over and said, as usual, "Well?" For some reason, I blew up. He always expects me to start the conversation, as if I were a phonograph. He was astonished at my flare-up and asked, "What do you mean by saying, 'I must be more careful with you'? Does it mean that you are playing a game with me?" What could I tell him? That he's a fool? I said that I would not explain or try to justify myself. Then he asked, "Then, perhaps, we ought to end this comedy?" I was silent. And he left. I followed him with my eyes for a long time. He did not turn. Now I will go to the pay station and call him. I wanted to keep my pride, but I see that I can't. I long for him. . . .

I went out and called him. He was out. I walked along the boulevard till the Arbat and back. And tried again. Again he was not home. Then I went walking along the streets he usually takes to go home. I thought we might meet. No, we did not meet. I came home. The walk calmed me down a little, but I still cannot do my schoolwork. What shall I do? I think that he no longer loves me and looks for faults in me. I have many faults, but I did not deserve the accusation that I "play a game." It is an insult. Perhaps we shall become friends again?

Exams are beginning. I am afraid that Lena will not be admitted: she has "poor" in algebra and physics.

May 19

Today we went to Lena's to study. Before Grisha came, I read her diary. Confused, excited entries in the beginning, then calmer ones. She has realized that she loves Grisha as a friend, just as she loves me. She decided not to leave school. I was glad to read that. We sat over our schoolwork till evening, then went walking. With Grisha, there's total peace.

May 20

Eleven in the evening. I've just come from the bank of the Moskva River. We've become very fond of that spot. I sat on a rock, and he stood before me, terrified that I might fall. After this evening, I feel so warm and full of joy. How good he is!!! He was talking about our boys. What a bunch of nasty scoundrels. The things he told me about them. . . .

I sat on the rock and recalled the Volga.

> Many songs have been sung of the Volga,
> But the tunes of those songs were not gay.
> In the old days our sorrow was singing,
> It's our joy that is singing today.
>
>> Our own, beloved, beautiful,
>> As bounteous as the sea,
>> Free as our own homeland,
>> Wide, deep and strong and free . . .

But if you listen closely, this song is also a pensive one. And always, whenever you are alone on the banks of the Volga, alone, even on a bright, sunny day, a kind of melancholy, not sadness, but a pleasant melancholy steals into your heart. Ah, how I long for the Volga, but not alone—with him. . . . I am tired of Moscow and its tactless people. Either you hear obscenities, or you're pushed, or someone swears for no good reason. . . .

We had a telegram from papa today. He is going directly to Khvalynsk, where we are to meet him. We're going to the Volga, and Nastya, the devil, doesn't write!

May 21

Today I went to the dentist and ran into Fishberg. "Why have you forgotten me?" Go to hell, I thought, to myself. "Perhaps you'll come up, or call me?" "No," I said, "I'll neither come nor call!" and walked away from him. He followed me. "Why so?" "I do not wish to give you any explanations!" Luckily they called him in, or he would have gotten a real tongue-lashing from me. Nasty creature!

May 22

Yesterday Grisha called and invited me for a walk. I refused, saying I was going to study. But two hours later I called him myself. I waited for him on the boulevard and watched the children. I love children. . . .

Then we went wandering through the streets without aim or direction. It began to rain. We hid under a canopy and stood there for a long time without speaking. And silently we said to one another more than we could have said with words. He took my hand and pressed it hard.

And at home, unexpectedly, there was something terrible and beyond understanding. My lost Uncle Misha was back. It turned out that he had come to Moscow to seek protection for his brother, arrested in Baku. He had gone to the NKVD to ask for justice and protection, and there he was arrested. Now he looks altogether confused and frightened. He was telling us about the shocking goings-on in Baku and kept looking over his shoulder and talking in whispers. At the NKVD they kept him all these days, and when they let him go, they advised him to keep quiet about his brother. In the evening, the family had a celebration—at least, he is free. We sang "In the Wild Steppes Beyond Baikal." Grandmother started crying. I went to the other room, feeling terribly sad. Now they are singing "Glorious Sea, Sacred Baikal" once again. I love that song. Papa sings it especially well. . . . Soon, soon I shall see him at last. . . .

May 23

Hurrah, the geometry test is over! I got through it quickly and well. Lena must have flunked. She did the problem, but bungled the theorem. She came out of class and burst into tears. We walked with her a while and calmed her.

In the evening we went to see parachute jumping. Magnificent!

And before that I was at Lena's and had a fight with her father. He said it was Lena's own fault that she flunked geometry. I told him it was his fault—why didn't he let her come to my house to study? Lena told me some awful things about her father.

May 25

Lena was at my house yesterday. She telephoned Grisha, and he came. But he left soon—he did not want to see Zunka, who is teaching me to ride a bicycle. He teaches me, and Grisha sulks. Why can't he be like everybody else—calm and simple?

My diary is ending. I've become so fond of this small, convenient copybook. I think of another with cold hostility. For two years I've confided my thoughts and feelings to my diary. . . . I have just reread it. A lot of childish nonsense, a lot of foolishness, but generally interesting.

I review my past like a moving picture film . . . Farewell, now you will go into my drawer. Years will go by, and perhaps, shaking the dust off your covers, I will sadly turn the yellowed pages, remembering and crying over my vanished youth. . . .

Second Copybook
[1938]

September 5

I meant to start from today, but then decided to tell about the past three months. They saw a sharp change in my whole life.

I passed the tests very well, with a single "good" in algebra, and "excellent" in all the other subjects. Exams were over, but we stayed on and on in Moscow. Papa had written that he would go directly to Khvalynsk, but there was no news from him. After a while, I got bored and decided to go to work at a summer camp. The District Committee even assigned me a salary. Grisha and I said good-bye for the summer like two people who love each other.

The conditions in camp stunned me from the very first days. The work turned out to be dreadfully difficult. Children are a capricious lot, and you must have iron nerves to work with them. In the beginning, I even used to cry. And I was not the only one to find things so hard. Kolya was also struggling. Our common work and our common sorrows and tribulations brought us together and made us friends. At first, he was friendly with Akhmetov and Shulgin, but later he had fights with them. I said to him: "You must remember, Kolya, that you have no friends here among the kids, and can't have any, even among the Komsomol members. And remember—I am the only one you can rely on in difficult moments."

We were alone among the unorganized, undisciplined mass of kids. The director was an incompetent weakling, and his assistant Valya did not contribute much either.

And the Komsomol members Akhmetov and Shulgin behaved worse than the Pioneers, demoralizing them and disrupting our work. During the first camp term, Zhora Zhivov was the only one who did some work or, to put it more exactly, did not interfere with work.

Disrupting of assembly, running off to the football field, parties till one in the morning, indecent songs— these were the usual things for Shulgin and Akhmetov. Toward the end Shulgin behaved altogether shamelessly. His affair with Shura Fedorova was known throughout the camp and threatened to end in a big, nasty scandal. I've literally come to hate those filthy fellows, especially Akhmetov.

I knocked myself out working with the first group. My unit had twenty Oktyabryata, most of them boys, regular demons. From one school they sent us the worst brats. . . . This whole first term was like an ugly nightmare.

I was glad when I was sent to Moscow two days before closing of the term to collect the clothing of the second group.

But when I came home, the first news I heard was like a hammer blow: papa had been arrested.

My head reeled, I went frantic and wrote Lena such a raving letter that she burned it immediately. At home we all felt as though we were about to be overrun by some ruthless invader.

I decided to return to camp, now with a definite aim: we needed money.

The senior camp leader this time was Nikolay Mazia—a wonderful fellow. He established good discipline from the first, and work became easy. Of the older kids, only Zhivov and Lukianov were left for the second term. Lukianov became my assistant, and Zhivov worked with the first squad, under Lesha.

I had twenty-five kids in my unit, and it was a pleasure to work with them. It was only this work and my children that saved me from black despair and total confusion over what had happened to my father.

I've gotten to love many of the children and will remember them for a long time, perhaps always. That darling Galochka—the tiniest human being in our camp, a little girl in a red dress. A pink little round face, huge eyes. Flitting around like a bit of flame. The favorite of the whole camp, and also of Kolya Mazia. But when Kolya would call her over to pat her on the head she'd come running to me, crying, "I want Nina, I love Ninochka!" I became terribly fond of her too.

In the previous group my favorite was Zhenya, another little one. But no, they've all grown dear to me, and I see a whole throng of faces now. I remember them all, all their names and characters, and I recall none of them with anything but affection.

Ella, Sveta, Maya—my star children, who left the camp with two pins on their chests and with presents. Vova, who was transferred to the Pioneers. And Kolya of the first group—a yellow-eyed little Tartar boy, with his slow, plaintive songs.

I remember one night by a fire. I was sitting alone in the woods, and Kolya, Yura, and Vova were sleeping in a small tent. About sixty paces away was the larger tent of the second unit. Akhmetov, Zhivov, and all the rest were there. They were noisy and gay; our tent was silent. I sat so throughout the night, my solitude disturbed only by the sentries who patrolled the area with sticks, "guarding" our tents. They came, ate some baked potatoes, and went away again into the dark, mysterious, listening woods. They were a little frightened, but manfully concealed it—brave, good kids!

I recall a swarthy, black-eyed little boy in red trunks, with an Eastern cast to his features. He drew very well, but he often cried. The children did not mistreat him, they were fond of him, but they kept him awake with their mischief, and he would cry, hiding his face in the pillow. I was very fond of him. In the first group, he and Zhenya were my favorites. He stayed at the camp two months, and I had no difficulty with him at any time. A dear boy and a good artist. He filled almost an entire album with his excellent sketches.

I was treated very well. Some of the fellows even called me "Ninochka," not to speak of the girls.

But the return to Moscow ended everything, all the peace I had during the summer. First of all, Lena was in trouble. She took repeat exams in physics and geometry and flunked again. She was left in the same class for a second year. I went to see Tatyana Alexandrovna and burst out crying while I talked to her. With Grisha, we had a heart-to-heart talk and decided that we were and would remain good friends.

September 7

What an ominous darkness has shrouded my whole life. Father's arrest is such a blow that it bends my back. Until now I have always carried my head high and with honor, but now . . . Now Akhmetov can say to me, "We're comrades in misfortune!" And just to think how I despised him and despised his father, a Trotskyite. The nightmare thought oppresses me day and night: is my father also an enemy? No, it cannot be, I don't believe it! It's all a terrible mistake!

Mother is calm and steadfast. She tries to reassure us; she is forever going somewhere, writing to someone, and feels sure that the misunderstanding will soon be cleared up.

At school everything is well. I told our new Komsomol organizer, Nina Andreyevna, about the situation in my family. She consoled me and advised me to keep up my spirit, not to despair. I was assigned a Pioneer unit again, although I protested emphatically, pointing to my situation. I frequently go to the District Committee to attend courses for group leaders, which takes up a great deal of time.

To escape gloomy thoughts and moods, I recall the past summer, the camp, and my little friends. Grisha wrote me seldom, and I did not like his letters. He does not know how to write letters. Separation is the truest test of human relations. When I realized that I was thinking more of Lena than of Grisha, I decided that I had simply gone through an ordinary girlish infatuation last spring. I was freed of this infatuation by the country environment, work with the children, association with other Komsomol members, and father's arrest. I suddenly felt very lonely without father's strong hand to lean on.

It's night now. In camp, it was the best time. We had one especially lovely spot there—a little wooden bridge on the way to the village of Aksenka. Our elbows on the railing, we looked at the moon and the falling stars, and listened to the distant crowing of village roosters. Frogs croaked in the little lake below, and crickets chirped tirelessly in the grass. It seemed that we—just two or three boys or girls—were alone in the whole world. And we were caught up in a strange, inexpressible feeling of sadness, of longing for something forever lost or unattainable, a restless expectation of something—perhaps some sorrow, or some joy. . . . Night rewarded us for the busy, noisy day.

And now I feel as though a rope were tightening around my throat. Such despair comes over me that I have no strength to shake myself, to unbend my back and look people boldly in the eye. To take a deep and joyous breath. . . .

September 10

Desolation and gloomy silence at home. Nobody is doing anything. Grandmother cries all the time—our father was her favorite son-in-law. After all, he was a friend of our grandfather, her husband, who died in the Civil War. After grandfather's death, father never broke his ties with the family. He married mama soon afterward, while he was still fighting. To top it all, there is no news of Uncle Ilyusha. He should have been here from Transbaikal by now, but he has disappeared. We have decided that he was probably arrested too.

Mama is looking for work. With father here, we never knew want. Now everything is falling to pieces. . . .

I have no one to share my troubles with. It seems to me that Lena is too preoccupied with some problems of her own, but she does not confide in me. She has become secretive and draws away from me into her own world like an oyster into its shell.

And I am sunk in a deep, gnawing depression. Everything is either repulsive or meaningless. Yesterday, Lena, Zhora, and I saw *On the Banks of the Neva* at the Maly Theatre. It was a very good play, and the acting was good, but I watched it with cold indifference.

I think I shall probably have a fight with Grisha soon. We are both to blame. He is closer with Lena, and calls me "Ninka." And I flare up at every word I don't like. The cleavage between us is widening and deepening.

That is my character: at night I'll cry and curse myself for my rudeness and quick temper, and in the morning I'll be still sharper and more rude. A savage character.

. . . Somebody told me that both my appearance and my character are Asiatic. I think it's true.

I remember father's stories about our ancestors on his side. His great-grandfather, a serf, a man of enormous strength, escaped from serfdom and joined a band of brigands. One day, as he was making his way to the Don, he was captured. He fought so hard that he broke one man's arm as though it were a stick, and twisted another's, almost tearing it out of the joint. Nevertheless, in the end he was tied up, and, after a whipping that left him nearly dead, he was delivered to his mistress. The lady was, evidently, a match for her serf. She broke him down to the point where he became . . . her executioner whenever she wished to punish any of his fellow villagers.

Father's grandfather was also a strong, unbending man. He married a girl who was one of the household serfs. When their mistress sent for his wife one day—she was the best lacemaker on the estate—my great-grandfather would not allow her to go. Then the lady summoned him: "Why don't you let your wife come when I call her?" "She is my wife and has to look after the house and the children." The mistress had an executioner, a woman, my great-grandfather's aunt. Her blow used to fell the strongest peasants. The lady ordered her to punish her disobedient nephew, and his aunt punched him so hard that he reeled. But he stayed on his feet and took a swing at her that knocked her out cold and sent her flying into the corner. Then he pulled a chisel from the leg of his boot (he was a carpenter) and started brandishing it until he chased all the gentry and their household out of the house and yard. After that, the mistress left him alone.

Our own grandfather, my father's father, was also rebellious in his youth. He set fire to the manor house after quarreling with his landowner over the workers' wages, and almost choked the estate manager to death. He took part in the revolution of 1905 and in the Civil War.

Father used to say, half-joking, that we have stormy Slavic blood with a Tartar streak. "Yes, we're Scythians . . . with slanting, greedy eyes. . . ."

And now all the young Kosterins—my father and Uncle Misha—are supposedly enemies of the people. How can I, their daughter in flesh and blood, believe this?

September 13

Lena spoke to me about herself. Grisha had said to her, "I tore the old love out of my heart with the roots, and I love you—but it is not a great love." Lena accepted it and wrote him a letter, saying that she loves him. I involuntarily burst out laughing and told Lena that it was nonsense—a man could not so easily stop loving one girl and begin to love another. Whoever tells a girl that he loves her "a little"? Grishka is an idiot, and Lena does not understand that he is simply "playing a game."

September 14

Yesterday we had a Komsomol meeting. We took up

Myron's application for membership, on Grisha's recommendation. Grisha gave him the highest praise, and Zhora already asked, "Who is in favor?" when I stopped him and demanded that we hear some other people on the question. Shurka began to tug me by the sleeve. "Everything's all right, my fair marquise!" But I took the floor and spoke very heatedly. I was supported by Zhora, and Myron was accepted only as a candidate for membership. "Why increase the number of bad members in our organization?" I argued. And attacked those who behaved disgracefully in camp. I called Shulgin a "brazen type." Akhmetov was sitting pale with rage. No, our fathers may both be in prison, but I'm no comrade of yours!

I've learned to be a good speaker, I am not afraid of audiences, and the words seem to pour out of themselves in strong, effective phrases.

September 16

Akhmetov and Shulgin greet me most cordially. And I've set to work with my unit with the greatest of energy.

Yesterday I had a serious talk with my kid sister Lelya. Mama had been called to school because of her conduct. Mama got upset and cried. In the evening, when I came home from school, I had a talk with Lelya. I told her how difficult it is for our whole family now because of papa's arrest. Our situation is so bad that she may have to go to work after the seventh year instead of continuing school. Lelya burst out crying. And her whole crime was that she threw a flower at the teacher!

Today I went to the reading room to study German, but it was closed. I decided to telephone Grisha. He asked me to come. I went, but was sorry I did: his mother met me with such cold hostility! She just barely squeezed out the words, "How do you do?" And after study, he did not even see me home as he used to. This isn't even friendly.

September 18

I've just come from the reading room. I sat for three hours reading Lenin and Lunacharsky. I like working in the reading room more and more.

September 20

Had a long talk with Lena yesterday about many things, and of course about Grisha. It hurts me that he seems to stress, as though deliberately, that we are no more than friends. He speaks to me only about trifles, and clearly avoids me. Lena is tired of his game. She has lately fallen under Tamara's influence. A few days ago they both stayed away from school—they were late, and spent all day at Tamara's. Lena's mother came to school and raised a commotion. Everybody got upset and there was an ugly row. Tatyana Alexandrovna also scolded Lena. What a weakling she is, and how easily she lets herself be influenced by people like Tamara—a girl who dreams of nothing but an empty, lightweight, tinselly life. And I am very fond of Lenka, I love her with a kind of special warmth. I cherish a secret hope that we'll be friends all our lives. I used to think we were very different, but now I think we are very much alike, despite all differences.

Yesterday I had a lovely surprise: one of my camp favorites, Ella, sent me a letter. She moved me almost to tears with her curlicues!

September 25

I've decided to go to the stadium every free day. Yesterday I spent four hours there—running, jumping, rowing, riding a bicycle, and throwing grenades. I passed in rowing and high jumps. I had an excellent time.

In the evening I telephoned Grisha to find out about our assignments. We got to talking, and he offered me his bicycle. I thanked him. . . .

September 26

What a fool I am, how I despise myself for calling Grisha—twice in a row. Of course he was home, but they told me he was out. He's probably thinking, "What a pest!"

And today he suddenly handed me a note offering his friendship, as he sees that I "do not have enough" friends. At first I almost burst into tears, then I flew into a rage and wrote him a rude and sharp reply.

And still another unpleasantness: Lena is leaving our school. Her father transferred her to another one. I got dreadfully upset. . . .

Generally, I am in a terrible state of mind. Something is badly wrong with me lately. We're studying chloroform in chemistry, and I had a sudden nasty little thought: it would be good to put an end to everything all at once. I quickly stopped myself, forced myself to think about something else.

October 2

Autumn. Foggy drizzle and mud. Where is papa now? How is he?

Someone is playing melancholy, mournful music on a violin. I think of these desolate days of my life. I have not lived yet, but I keep thinking: is there any sense in going on?

My friendships are breaking up.

The other day Zhorzhik, with whom I became very friendly in camp, telephoned and we went walking. But I behaved badly; I kept interrupting him, making cutting remarks, and insulting him for no reason at all.

My note to Grisha also made our break final. He is turning away from me. I feel that I could still make things right if I wanted. But I can't. I seem to do everything as if to spite myself. I approach him intending to say one thing and say the opposite. What is this? Why?

I feel sorry for Zhorzhik too. I want to take him by

the shoulders and ask him, like a friend, not to abandon me. I offended him badly, but I cannot do anything to restore our relations.

Lena has been at the new school for two days. She likes it there. I miss her very much. All these days I feel with particular sharpness that I have no one else, that she is my only friend. . . . And she is far away!

Yesterday we had a Komsomol meeting. A whole discussion flared up about Kiryak, a fellow who is slippery as an eel, with a wolf's cunning and the unscrupulousness of a speculator. A Komsomol member, too! Several people, including myself, spoke against him. But he came out whitewashed. "There are no facts, Nina, and facts are stubborn things!" he said to me after the meeting. He has chosen a suitable profession—law. He cleverly parried all charges and cleared himself. It turned out that he was the finest and noblest member of the organization. A shifty, slippery man. One of our writers called such people "cephalopods." An octopus! When he is a lawyer, he may become a dangerous enemy of our Socialist society.

October 7

There's a stony weight in my chest. In such a mood I don't have much control of myself and may do something bad. I went to see Tatyana Alexandrovna. She told me things that convinced me even more what a vile, nasty creature I am.

Yesterday I called Grisha and asked him to come to the reading room. He came. Then he walked me home.

And today he telephoned and we went bicycle riding. He is very calm. I did not notice any agitation in him . . . or any feelings.

There were moments yesterday when a heavy, empty silence fell between us. Between friends silence is often more expressive than words. With us, there is only emptiness. But why does it trouble me so? After all, I repulsed him. Or am I really a monster who tries to get a man to fall in love only to repel him rudely? Tatyana Alexandrovna is right in suspecting that I have some very bad traits. But all of this is not intentional, I do not want to do what I am doing. Why, then, does it turn out like this? It sometimes even frightens me . . .

I told Grisha that I needed friendship, and therefore rejected his love. Before I sat down to my diary I said to myself, "I love him." But was afraid to write it down, because it would lead immediately to "I don't love him." What is he: a toy, a rubber ball? I may be losing something great and significant, but I must step aside.

What am I living for? What is ahead for me? It is frightening to think that so much suffering has come to me in just a few short months, and that it's breaking me up so badly. And time crawls like a long sleepless night —a sticky, tormenting night without rest. . . .

By chance, I came across his poem, written last spring:

> Tonight an autumn wind is howling,
> Blinding my eyes with rain.
> Today, for the last time, we parted,
> With final words, not to be heard again . . .

I am reading these words, and tears fall on the page . . .

October 8

If you knew how grateful I am to you! A small token of attention—but how happy it made me! Yesterday he invited me to use his bicycle, and today he reminded me again—I can take his bicycle and go riding with Zhorzhik. But I refused. Truly, there is some devil in me, and it won't let me live in peace.

I've read Goethe's *Tasso*. The poet Tasso says to Eleonora that his words and actions contradict his wishes. Whole strophes pour into my mind and remain in my memory without any effort:

> Oh, if there were only some among you
> Who knew how to value women,
> Who could discern and fathom
> The purest treasure
> Of love and faithfulness
> Concealed in woman's heart . . .

October 9

Yesterday I was in the reading room with Grisha. I was reading Blok. I liked the epigraph to his article on "Irony":

> I do not like your irony.
> Leave it to those who've finished living or who
>   haven't lived.
> It's not for you and me, who have loved so
>   passionately,
> Who still retain a remnant of the feeling—
> It is too early for us to indulge in it.
>   [NEKRASOV]

Today we wandered over Moscow. I suddenly said, "I am sometimes afraid to understand myself." He asked what I meant. I did not want to explain—I am afraid of going into intimacies.

Lately I've developed a love for poetry. I read poems aloud to an involuntary listener—my kid sister Lelya. She listens, but does not understand either the poems or me!

> What if the moon be bright—the night stays dark.
> Life may bring others joy—
> Within my soul the spring of love
> Will not replace the howling storm.

I recently read H. G. Wells's *Love and Mr. Lewisham.* Ethel! What a good description of the beginning, the walks, the birth of love. From all of that I realized how careful one must be when marrying. Heaven prevent one from stepping, like Ethel, into a vacuum! Poor Mister! He had dreadfully bad luck in life: such noble aspirations and such a sad end.

Wells's view is that it was his own fault. Life is a game.

October 15

At last I can take a rest. I've just conducted an assembly devoted to the twentieth anniversary of the Komsomol. It went well, and the kids are pleased. Our play, *Under a Mask of Loyalty*, was praised by everyone. Kolya played beautifully—he's a born actor. The others were also pretty good. Zhenya and Akhmetov accompanied and were a great help. Our audience consisted of parents. Nina Andreyevna and Valya also came. Everybody enjoyed it very much.

Grisha is working on the newspaper. It must be out October 17th, but nothing is ready. I miss Grishka, we haven't had any walks for a long time—he is too busy, or, to be more exact, he doesn't want to. I love him now! Yesterday, the day before yesterday, today! Perhaps there will be days when I'll think of him with irritation, but now I love him, I love him!

October 19

The day before yesterday we had a concert. The performers—Chechen and Ingush students from the conservatory, and an orchestra. Grisha's paper came out at the very last moment. He missed the whole evening. I went home with Lena and Petya. At the bus stop Grisha caught up with us. I walked with him until three in the morning.

Yesterday we were at the reading room. I read Goethe; he did his lessons.

Strange—despite all the tension in my life and all my moods, my marks are excellent, and my activities are going well . . .

October 24

On October 22nd we had committee elections. I waited for the day with trepidation. Of course I wanted to be elected, but I was sure I'd either lose or be disqualified.

During discussion of the slate, I declared myself disqualified, in view of my father's arrest. However, Akh-metov (his father was arrested too) was disqualified, but I was left. In the balloting, I received 29 votes out of 34! Grisha was the only one who outstripped me—30 votes! The rest drew only 24, 25. In the allocation of duties, I was assigned to mass cultural work.

October 25

Yesterday I had a little run-in with Glebova, and this gave me the idea of describing the girls in our class.

The Customs and Characters of the Tenth Class

In the tenth class there are no friendships between girls and boys. It cannot be said that they avoid each other, that they don't talk or play together. But the lives of the boys and girls somehow run along separate channels. The boys seem to form a more homogeneous group, and I would find it difficult at present to divide them into sub-groups. But the girls I divide into three groups: "the bog," "the young ladies," and "Komsomol members."

"The bog" is Svetlova and her company. "The young ladies" are Glebova and two other girls. Few of the girls of "the bog" are good students, but they have no other interests either. School does not excite them; public life is something they neither understand nor have any inter-est in. At school they gossip; at home, they also seem to care about nothing but gossip of the kitchen and market-place variety. They tag after "the young ladies" and envy them secretly: "Why can't I be like that?" If they could, they would become "young ladies." But some of them—like Semenova and Mikhailova—could probably be gotten out of "the bog" and brought into the Komsomol. The fact that they are in "the bog" is unquestionably the fault of our Komsomol group. As for Svetlova, she is a lump of solid, dull obstinancy; and Fedorova is an ideal example of stupidity.

The "young lady" Glebova. Hair curled, briefcase handle torn. Sticks at the hairdresser's for two hours, but has no time to do her lessons. "It's disgraceful to walk on low heels at our age!" If you say, "Perhaps Tosya has other ideas of what is disgraceful," she snaps at you rudely. "I'm not talking to you!" Pays little attention to the boys in her class, or, rather, of her age. She aims higher. Svetlana Glebova wants a life "lived so beautifully that you'll have something to look back on" (it's easy to guess what "beauty" means to her). Ogloblina calls the boys asses and idiots, but has nothing else on her mind than being liked by them. Hair fluffed up (a permanent), stocking torn, narrow skirt (latest style!), circle of interests as narrow as her skirt. Of "the young ladies," I like Galya best. If she could be torn away from Olya and Lisa and their influence, she could become a decent human being.

Our own group of Komsomol girls is closer to the boys. Our relations with them are friendly. Some of the Komsomol girls are influenced by "the bog" and "the young ladies." Katya is a good and intelligent girl, but with a tendency to excessive liberalism. Dolginskaya is intelligent and straightforward, but she is much too concerned with permanents, nail polish, narrow skirts. . . .

October 27

Night. Silence. The din of Moscow is quieting down. Time to sleep, but I have Gorky's "Grandfather Arkhip and Lyonka" before me. Read half a page, and hurried to get my diary. I can see them so vividly, so clearly: the grandfather and the boy on the bank of the Kuban. And immediately, my own memories—the luxuriantly green banks of the Volga near Khvalynsk, the white sandy shoals. . . . Perhaps I shall never again see that magnificent river, but I shall never forget our little adventures there—simple, but heartwarming and marvelous.

Lelya, father, the artist Kolya, and I in a rowboat, on a long trip "around the world" (around the island). Night on a sandbar. A brightly flaming bonfire. Fiery reflections dancing on the waves. The Volga, vast and mighty, carrying its waters to the distant sea. A steamship glittering with lights appears from around the bend of the river, plows up the Volga noisily, and disappears in the distance. And the only thing that stirs the air is the light breeze, bringing a mournful musical phrase across the Volga, a fragment of a melancholy song. . . . And father starts quietly:

> Come out upon the Volga—who is moaning
> Over the mighty Russian river, lost to hope?
> In our land we prefer to call it singing—
> It is the boatmen pulling on their rope. . . .

And then the astonishing dawn, with scarlet glints flashing and dimming over the river's vast expanse. We worked hard, rowing, and only Kolya never touched either oar or pole. I remember papa whispering in my ear: "Kolya is a gentleman, he is afraid of blistering his delicate hands. . . ."

I also remember how the three of us, papa, Lelya, and I, hauled our boat upstream. There was a strong wind blowing. It was impossible to row against both wind and current, and we had to walk along the bank, pulling the boat with a rope. For a while I walked along the river, shivering, wet to the bone, constantly stumbling into pits and gulleys. Then papa relieved me and pulled until my conscience would speak up: he would never be the first to admit fatigue. . . . Often father took us fishing. We brought along fishing rods, bread, and potatoes, and went off far, far away. We'd build a fire, but papa never trusted us to bake the potatoes. It was a sacrosanct procedure, and he insisted on performing it himself; with the most earnest expression, he would rake away the ash and arrange the potatoes. . . . And our outings in woods and in orchards, and those six days in the rowboat on the Volga—three hundred kilometers! I shall never forget those two years on the Volga . . . or my father. . . .

But let me go back to "Grandfather Arkhip and Lyonka" . . .

October 30

I once had a girl friend Panka. This was a time when I chose the worst girls in class as my friends. Katka, Panka, Valka, Sima . . . I was closest with Panka. Stubborn as a devil. She'd be called to the blackboard, but the teacher couldn't get a word out of her. She knew her lesson, but she wouldn't speak. Of our entire company, she was the most hostile toward boys. She never talked to them except to quarrel and call names, and they had no other name for her but "pikey." And she looked like a pike too: skinny, with a long, pointed nose and a wide mouth. We had a whole group of such girls, and I was the ringleader. We were all poor students. I was the best, but I never got beyond "satisfactory." My group took no part in social activities and spent every recess fighting with the boys. We'd fight as a close unit, all together. In class, we sat in the last rows and talked all the time. At school, we did not use bad language, but outside we did our worst; we rang bells, rode hanging onto streetcars and trucks, spouted obscenities. Those were our favorite occupations. In the street, Panka was the most timid of the lot, but at school, her high, piercing voice was heard on every floor.

We shared the last desk in the back—at that time my eyesight was good. When my eyes got worse, I moved up closer front. Then my eyes got even worse. I asked her to move up with me, but she refused, and would not help me read the blackboard. Then I left her and moved to a front desk.

In all matters pertaining to everyday life, Panka was worldlier, more experienced, than I. I was utterly naïve and foolish. Panka often rolled with laughter, explaining all kinds of obscenities to me. We never flirted with the boys. We thrashed them—that was the extent of our relations.

Panka was noisy and shrill, forever chattering away.
She was very concerned about her appearance, but her
home was dirty and neglected. She was bad at school and
dropped out in the seventh class. After she went to work,
her appearance began to change. Her hat was no longer
down on her forehead—it sat at a jaunty angle. She curled
her hair, wore stylish dresses, used lipstick. And, generally, she filled out and became prettier. Even her bow
legs straightened out. I warned her not to slip down into
the streets, but she would only shrug, "Who d'you think
you're talking to, Nina?"

This evening I went to see her. She was out, working.
I stayed a while, talking to her mother. Her mother is a
coarse, loud-voiced woman. She swears obscenely, with
indecent gestures. And complains about Panka, "Scum,
mangy bitch, she ought to . . ." She says that Panka calls
her "psycho" and gives her no money.

Their room is filthy, with a curiously stale, sour smell,
disgusting. There's one bed, and everybody sleeps in it
together. Instead of a pillowcase, there is a dirty striped
piece of rag over the pillow. That's how Panya lives.
But she dresses well, with a kind of vulgar chic. Lives
like an animal.

I asked for a piece of paper. After a long search, her
mother finally dug up a scrap, a corner off a map. I left
a note asking Panya to drop in.

Why did I go there? It's interesting to see what becomes of her. I do not want to see her often, but it
wouldn't be bad to observe her. I am sorry for Panka—
she is rolling down a steep incline. Once we were friends,

both of us wild, unruly kids, yet how sharply our roads have parted, how much divides us now!

Lena came to see me today. Then we went to visit Tatyana Alexandrovna. On the way from her, we picked up Grisha and went to the Museum of Fine Arts. I love this museum. I first came there with father, and ever since I feel good there.

Yesterday Grisha walked me home, but refused to come in. I pulled him and scolded him, and he said, "How pretty you are when you're angry!" He has such fine eyes—blue, intelligent . . .

And our family is still pursued by a host of evil spirits. We received a letter from Uncle Ilya. He is in prison, and asks us to send him a parcel. Grandmother is upset, mama is angry and berates us as if we were to blame. She also rages at father. . . . And I have not a shadow of doubt that he is innocent.

October 31

I am reading Gorky's *The Orlovs*. I love Gorky. I read and reread him, and then read him again.

Yesterday I read Blok's "The Intelligentsia and the Revolution" and " 'Religious Questing' and the People." "The Russian intelligentsia is deaf—as though a bear had stepped on its ear. Petty alarms, petty words. Isn't it shameful to make fun of illiterate announcements or letters written by a good but clumsy hand? Isn't it shameful to answer 'stupid questions' with proud silence? Isn't it shameful to pronounce the beautiful word 'comrade' with quotation marks?

"With your whole body, your whole heart, your whole mind—listen to the Revolution."

That's strongly said!

November 1

I have a strange premonition of still more disasters in our family. I often dream about father. I did last night. It seemed that he came home—a gloomy stranger, and . . . wearing a tie. He never dressed like that. I woke, and felt so bitterly wretched, I could have howled like a wolf . . .

November 2

The only peace I find is in books. I fill every free moment with reading. Just finished Upton Sinclair's *No Pasaran*.

November 4

He told me directly that he does not love me. More than that—he does not understand me. He suspects that I am in love with Kolya Shcheglov. Well, that's going too far! I once said that Shcheglov is one of those who are "born to crawl—never to fly." And suddenly Grisha serves up Shcheglov as the object of my love! I was furious, but decided to say nothing. Then, as though some imp had pulled me by the tail, I said: "Yes, I like him!" And Grisha went away completely sure it's true. And I love him, the fool!

But what am I to do? Tell him? How can I hang myself on him with my little "love"? No! I'd rather suffer, but I won't drag him into my emotional mess too. I'll try to bury myself in work and books, so I'll have less time for craziness.

My time, though, is filled up to the hilt anyway. In addition to school and Komsomol work, I've taken up tutoring—I'm helping a boy with his lessons, earning some money. I never get home before midnight.

I am reading Gorky's *The Lower Depths*. What a dreadful life. . . .

November 7

I recall Lena last spring. I'm just like that now. My tongue seems to be tied, my head doesn't work, I do everything as in a fog. I try to run around, work, read, but *that* never leaves my mind.

I've become a bore and I hate myself. I am sad, and he is gay. He laughs merrily and amuses the whole class. And I . . . even my laugh has become convulsive, hysterical. . . .

My only salvation is books and the theatre. I have read Anatole France. A very original writer. Sharp, terse language, great sense of humor. Satirizes the present, but does not visualize the future.

Attended *Faust* at the Bolshoi Theatre. At first I liked it. You must forget Goethe's *Faust*, then you will understand the *Faust* at the Bolshoi. Here Faust is a lecherous old man who made his pact with Mephistopheles only to return his youth. . . . The best thing in it is the music. Especially the arias "Men Perish for Base Metal," "Do Not Open the Door," the enchanting waltz, and many other places. Mephistopheles (Pirogov) is magnificent, Marguerite (Baratova) is a bit too old, Faust (Zhadan) a bit too fat. This spoils the impression.

November 20

The day before yesterday I saw *Lubov Yarovaya* at the Moscow Art Theatre. The plot isn't new, quite hackneyed, but the production is good. The character of Luba, a strong woman, is convincing and memorable.

Yesterday there was a meeting of the literary circle. Grisha came. I read Kozma Prutkov. I was keyed up, and both my talk and my reading went well. I was expressive, gay, and carried everyone along. My proposal about publishing a literary magazine was adopted. I was nominated for the editorial board, but I declined.

In the evening, Grisha phoned and invited me to his house. Lena was there. I went. The streets were white with fresh, gay snow, but when I came, my tongue seemed to stick to my palate. On the way home I relaxed a little and became livelier. Lena doesn't understand what's wrong with me and scolds me.

November 25

Was at the Red Army Theatre. *The Philistines.* A very strong play. A good deal in our lives is still as it was in the lives of the "Philistines," though Gorky's play was written long ago. We must fight philistinism, and I will fight it. Not only limited, trivial, stupid people, but also intelligent and cultivated ones can sink into the bog of petty-bourgeois, philistine ways.

November 26

Our Komsomol organizer Nina Andreyevna is all right! We want to make a revolution at school—kick out the director. The brazen nerve: he has an apartment, but he's appropriated three rooms at school for his own use as well. He's quite a type, our director.

November 27

I feel as if I had taken a cold, refreshing shower.
Today Grisha and I went to see Nina Andreyevna. The conversation went as usual nowadays: he talks, and I am silent. I don't know what the devil it is: I seem to get petrified, my tongue is tied, and all of me gets frozen. When Grisha left, I got to talking with Nina Andreyevna. She told me about herself, her school, her mother. I admire her, she is becoming the ideal woman to me. She spoke to me frankly: one of my faults is lack of sensitivity to people; I try to make everyone fit my demands

without considering the person's individual capacities and character. I told Nina Andreyevna about my pessimistic thoughts and my feelings in connection with father and with my own personal affairs. She said that I behave stupidly, that one should not abandon oneself to the whims of fate. One must build one's own life. Nothing drops from the sky of itself, it is necessary to fight for life. She also told me that I am "in love with Grisha."

We walked through the streets for almost two hours. Dear Nina Andreyevna! After the talk with her I felt as if a great burden had fallen from my shoulders.

December 5

Books and the theatre are increasingly becoming my best friends.

In two weeks, I saw: Dunayevsky's operetta, *The Golden Valley*. Unsuccessful. The plot, the music, the characters are all mediocre.

Boris Godunov at Stanislavsky's Theatre. Extraordinarily strong impression. Especially the scenes at the inn, with the holy fool, in the children's room. After *Boris* I took a special trip to the library to read up on Moussorgsky.

Saw *King Lear* at the Jewish theatre. Not knowing the language affected the impression. The production is good, the actors marvelous, but all the same it seems to me that Lear is much too Jewish! It would have been better in a Russian theatre.

Read Balzac—*A Woman of Thirty, Silhouette of a*

Woman, etc. Liked them at first, but in the end got tired of all those women of the world going crazy from nothing to do.

A very strong impression was left by Theodore Dreiser's *The Titan*.

[1939]

March 4

So much water gone under the bridge. So many rotten experiences in the past three months that my hand scarcely obeys me to write it down. . . .

Now I am working intensively: studying, reading, skating. . . . Anything, to have no free time.

I have tried to forget the things that happened, but I can't. I must calmly, without sparing myself, try to analyze everything, to prevent the recurrence of such days in the future.

Just another step, and I would have committed something utterly vile. Thank God I didn't. Thanks to Lena . . . When I was planning to do it, I did not even understand the whole meanness and baseness of the deed. And Svetlana (a nasty little soul!) was ecstatic: "Oh, how interesting it will be!" It's lucky I told this to Lena as though it were Svetlana's plan, not mine. Lena, dear girl, my only friend, warned me to stay away from Svetka's influence and to break with her before it was too late.

But let me describe everything in order.

Before vacation, and even during vacation, I was still a respected member of the committee, a Komsomol member with a good deal of authority. I had many comrades who treated me with affection and regard.

But when I returned to school after vacation and the long illness that followed, I felt lonely and isolated from the very first days. I found that a new girl student had taken the center of the class—an excellent and active Komsomol member.

At parties, Katya was surrounded by a crowd, and I was alone (with Svetlana). Grisha was also there. Some of the boys, seeing me alone, became rude. Oh, I had never before known the meaning of loneliness! Always and everywhere alone! I suffered dreadfully and withdrew into myself. . . . Only books and the theatre helped me a little.

And I became embittered, and anger suggested a way out. Svetka was also alone. Two "lonely and unhappy" souls found each other and formed an alliance. And our plan was this: to break up the group around Katya and create a circle of admirers around ourselves. To accomplish this, I was to confess my love to Petya and thus draw him away from Katya's retinue . . . then do the same with the other boys. I no longer realized what I was doing. Where were my honesty, my principles? I was consumed with envy—mean, nasty little envy of Katya.

All of this is behind me now. At the wretched party where I had intended to carry out my plan, I caught myself in time, had a fight with Svetka, and left. I walked home choking on my tears and cursing myself and Svetka.

But that evening marked a turning point. I could not fall asleep for a long time. But I found an answer: I must work and study, and the rest will come of itself. I am still ashamed of the past, terribly ashamed, but it will never happen again.

Now I am in a better mood. I read, I work with zest and enjoyment, and spend all my free time at the skating rink.

March 6

A tragicomic scene took place today.

Verochka was playing with her doll. I was ironing the wash. The coal in the iron went out and the iron got cold. I was tired of sorting the wash and I buried my nose in Feuchtwanger's *The False Nero*. And, as usual, I became so absorbed in reading that I forgot everything and did not see or hear anything around me. Then I broke away for a second—and, horrors! Verochka was sitting on the floor, next to her stood the iron, and she was munching away at the coal with the greatest delectation! Her whole face was black, only the eyes glittered. I screamed involuntarily (with fright), and Verochka ran away to the next room. With a mouth full of coal!

The noise brought mama from the kitchen and she had a good laugh over my fright. Let her eat! There must be something lacking in her organism, and the child hankers for coal.

March 8

My latest enthusiasm—Lion Feuchtwanger. I've never really known him until now. Had read only *The Oppermanns*. But the real Feuchtwanger isn't there; he's in *Josephus*. What an astonishing book! I could not tear myself away from it, I neglected my lessons and took it with me to school.

I set myself a task: to read all of Feuchtwanger and write a composition on "Feuchtwanger's Anti-Fascist Novels."

March 20

Didn't go to school today. Sat, reading. Suddenly . . . Seryozha Meshcheryakov! Papa's old childhood friend! But what is left of him! Ragged, dirty, drunk. Nothing but the voice remains. And his voice is marvelous. He sings beautifully, with deep, warm feeling. He has a good head too, he's an excellent mathematician—and look how low he has sunk!

Once Meshcheryakov wanted to give himself up to the Tsarist gendarmes in papa's place. Now he also cries and says that he would give his life for papa. I look at him,

and tears come to my eyes against my will—I pity him,
and I keep thinking of papa. And Seryozha suddenly
began to sing, but what a song, and how he sang it!

"The beautiful Greek Women on the Bosphorus . . ."

I burst into tears. Grandmother and mother after me.
Another picture rose so vividly before us: a room full of
papa's old friends, friends from the underground revolutionary days and the Civil War. And Seryozha Meshcheryakov singing:

> "Far away, far away,
> Beyond Volga the steppes . . ."

Seryozha seemed to understand me and started up this
song again. I have never heard Russian songs, the songs
of the Volga, sung with such feeling, such lyrical
depths. . . .

He's a good man, Seryozha, but a lost soul. Papa alone
could have rescued him from this morass of shiftless
drunkenness.

March 25

Vacation time, and I am disgustingly lazy.

I have just come from Lena. Grisha was there too. I
have been spending much time with Grisha lately, and
our relations are excellent. He told me that he had tried
to fool himself and me. He loves me. My feeling toward
him is also more than friendship. But it is altogether different now. Much calmer, but deeper and more serious.

I don't show it, though, and don't intend to. Let it be friendship.

I am sorry for Lena. I am happy, and she is lonely.

Hurrah! A telegram. Ilya is free and asks us to send him money for the fare.

There is rejoicing at home, but I think of father. . . .

March 27

Affairs at the Komsomol are in a bad state. In fact, the organization is demoralized. We need resolute action. Nina Andreyevna agrees with me, but warns against harsh measures. I am taking it up in earnest, we shall revive the organization.

How damned good life is, in spite of everything! I shall soon be eighteen! That's a lot, isn't it?

I am eighteen, I am loved, and I love!

Beautiful!

Third Copybook
[1939]

July 25

And so, allow me to introduce myself: Nina Alexe-yevna Kosterina, "five minutes away from being a college student," or—to put it more exactly—a "something" still hanging between heaven and earth.

It's more than a month since I graduated from school and now, like many others, I'm trying to get into a place where I seem to be "drawn by invisible powers"—the Institute of Geology. With torment and soul-searching, an "ordinary girl" took stock of her still unknown abilities: what can she be good for in life? She searched and now, as it seems to her, she found an answer. And my decision is firm and unshakable. Even if I fail the tests, I shall consider this year a test of myself. I shall work with geological expeditions as an ordinary worker and try again for my chosen goal next year.

The heady mists of spring in my head and my heart, the exams, the frequent walks with Grisha, the delirium of love—all of this has receded into a purple distance.

As in the past, I do not understand my relations with Grisha. Poor boy! I have tormented him unforgivably. . . . He writes:

I do not want to love you! But this begins the old, old story—the quarrel between head and heart. At times I love Lena very much, at other times I can't endure her. I tried to force myself to think that I loved her, and believed this self-deception.

But it was all a kind of defense against you. I closed my ears, I did not write to you, I did not think about anything. . . . At that time, when we spoke about Kolka, I deliberately kept repeating that I did not love you. It was self-delusion. Stupid, but what can you do. . . . Afterward, I used to take long walks. I suffered and suffered. And then I'd go rampaging, kidding around wildly. There were times when I longed to get drunk. In those days I struck up a friendship with Myron, and he often came to see me. At the same time, I turned feverishly toward Lena. I did not want to believe what you said about yourself, but everything you did convinced me that your words were true. . . .

And now I don't know what to do, what to think. I do not want to love you, but I do! I should not have taken you by the arm yesterday, but I did!

I never reproached you for your infatuation with Zhorzhik. And if you fall in love with someone else tomorrow, you will be right anyway. You shall never hear a single word of reproach from me. All those self-accusations that you are "a monster who tries" and so on are nonsense. The trouble is that none of it really carries you away completely, head and heart. . . .

Nina, Ninochka, Ninok, I love you. I love you as I always did! This is the only certainty out of all

this delirium. . . . A gypsy orchestra is playing behind me. My mood is like this music: I want to
dance, to cry and to laugh.

I see and I understand that my letter is like the
raving of a man in delirium. I hoped to find strong
words—vivid and convincing, but I see that everything I want to say is contained in three short words
—"I love you!"

I love! Whom do I love? I do not know,
But yet my heart glows warmly in my breast.
I whisper and I dream, repeating,
"Come, my beloved, come, my best . . ."

And here is another letter:

During one of those sleepless nights when time
seems endless, I was thinking . . . about you, of
course.

And these are the conclusions I came to. I have
very many faults; you do not notice all of them.
And therefore I must give you up. But I must do it
in a way that will be painless to you. And I? To the
devil with me! Why? Because I have loved you too
much. And still do! You will say this is absurd, but
to me the thought was heartwarming. You are
everything to me. I must never lie to you, under any
circumstances. And this was why I have often
placed myself in a stupid position—as a dull-witted
dandy, as mama's spoiled darling. . . . I wanted you
to stop loving me. But I was mistaken. . . . I mis-
judged you! You are sufficiently clear-minded and
clear-sighted, you are not a blind kitten.

I used to think: I don't deserve you because I
have loved already. And I must confess I've been
corrupted by it.

My dearest! If all this ever ends, I shall remember you always. This isn't a mere phrase. Your memory will be bright and pure. I compare my infatuations with Katya, Lena, and Alka with my present feeling. It's altogether different! This is a feeling I have never known. Do you remember, I quoted Lermontov? This applied to Lena, not to you. You, my beloved, are better, purer, and nobler than anyone else.

My loved one, take good care of yourself. . . . I kiss you with all my warmth (as once on the banks of the Moskva River).

And many poems. Strictly speaking, the poems are not too good. I am spoiled by the great poets—from Pushkin to those of our day. Nevertheless, I like Grisha's poems. Naturally, for they are dedicated to me. . . .

But what happened? Why these sudden letters?

It began—as important things often begin—with a trifle.

One day I came to Lena, and she invited me to dinner. Before I knew it, I was sitting at the table, eating borsch. On my right sat an old man I did not know—huge and fat. He kept saying that Lena was overfeeding him. He asked for smaller portions, and kept putting away double ones. And on my left. . . . The first thing I noticed was his mutilated left hand, then the voice—for some reason I liked it very much.

Soon afterward I was at Lena's again and met him a second time. I had almost no conversation with him, except for an exchange of a few insignificant phrases. I spent a marvelous day and left in the evening, but . . . I left my heart there. Who was he? Lyova, Lena's brother. Twenty years old, married, the head of a family. He is divorcing his wife. He does not love her, but he adores his daughter. That's all. And I love him.

I try to forget him, I try not to meet him. Of course I have no hope that he can ever return my feeling. But my thoughts are all about him. . . .

I study, I try to prepare for the tests, but I work so little that there's hardly any hope of being admitted to the Institute. I often go to the stadium, I am excited about football, running competitions, and so on. On the 20th there was a grandiose event at the stadium: a repetition of the physical culture parade. What majesty and beauty! And then I have become a swimming enthusiast.

All this takes up enormous amounts of time. This is how time is spent by this ordinary girl "on the brink" of college.

July 27

Books, theatre, movies—my good companions in life. By hook or by crook, often at the risk of a row with the ushers, I get into theatres. Books I pick up at random, without plan or system. This often makes me feel that my "brains are addled," "loaded with all sorts of trash."

Therefore it is necessary from time to time to try and bring some order into all the mass of facts, impressions, and moods my head is stuffed with. Perhaps arrange it all on little metal shelves, with labels (even if self-devised ones!), in the hope that sometime later, at leisure, I may make some sense of the material in my "storage room."

And so, what has come into my poor head during the past three months?

The most prominent place, of course, belongs to Mérimée. I liked his books enormously, especially *Carmen* and *Souls in Purgatory*. Next comes Conan Doyle. Exciting reading, yet it should of course be placed at some distance from Mérimée in my "storage room." I have also reread Pushkin, and whole strophes impressed themselves in memory without any effort on my part—probably for the rest of my life.

Accidentally, I made a "discovery": I "found" Sheller-Mikhailov in Russian literature, and I am enthusiastic about his books—*From Quagmire out onto the Highroad*, *Gilded Shame*, and others. How well he knew the behind-the-scenes life of high society, and how well he showed it.

One of the first places also belongs to *Old Times in Poshekhonye* by Saltykov-Shchedrin. I must make a mental note to read all the most important books of this writer.

And here is the music shelf: biographies of Rimsky-Korsakov, Mozart, Tchaikovsky, and Moussorgsky. My musical education does not go beyond rather mediocre playing on the guitar—father's present. But music always moves me strongly. I would like to develop a deeper understanding of this art.

I must also find room for such remarkable books as Victor Hugo's *Les Miserables*, Sergeyev-Tsensky's *Michel Lermontov*, Kuprin's *The Pit*, Bryusov's *Altar of*

Victory ... My poor head, where shall I find room for all this, and in what order? How can Mayakovsky live in the neighborhood of Afanasy Afanasievich Fet?

> At once I blotted out the map of everydays,
> Splashing paint on it from the glass. . . .

And side by side with it, Fet's lines:

> The sun's ray through the limes was a fiery band,
> You were tracing a pattern on glittering sand. . . .

I have tried to analyze all this and ended in total confusion. What are my tastes, then? Why do I delight in reciting Mayakovsky's

> I abhor all carrion!
> I adore all that's alive!

and then take as much pleasure in reading Esenin:

> You remember,
> You remember everything, of course. . . .

Or else I listen, moved, to mama singing Esenin's "Letter to My Mother":

> Still alive, my old, my dear one?
> So am I. I greet you from afar!
> May the gentle light of evening
> Flow upon you from the evening star. . . .

Heine, Esenin, Longfellow, Mayakovsky—I can read them one after the other with equal excitement. And they all live side by side within me like amicable tenants in a large apartment. But sometimes it seems to me that this amity is deceptive and threatens me with great difficulties, that it may already imperceptibly be undermining my psyche and my mind. . . . No, but this cannot be true—my pulse is full and strong, and I see my road clearly before me.

July 28

Only a few days are left before admission tests, but Nadya (my partner in the preparatory work) and I are not studying enough by far. Only six or seven hours a day, which is very little, especially if you have reviewed only half of the program. . . . And yesterday we went to Grisha, at Silver Wood, supposedly to study, and, naturally—as was to be expected—lost half a day.

August 1

Read *Letter From an Unknown Woman* by Stefan Zweig. O-oh, how it moved me, how it shook me. I wept over the letter. Then I thought of Lyova and began to cry over myself. What nonsense! I try to forget him. . . . And I am sure that I will laugh at myself after a month or two. In the meantime, I give myself up to such stupid feelings. . . .

August 2

Lena came to see me yesterday. When I was walking her home, we ran into Grisha. And, of course, we went

wandering through the streets. And behaved as stupidly
as usual when the three of us are together. I was fooling
around, kidding Grisha. Now wanting to take him by
the arm, now quarreling with him. Lena was furious because Grisha was not attentive to her. She loves him and
expects more than simple, friendly relations with him.
And he, the good-for-nothing, does not notice anything
—neither her pain, nor her love. Lena is generally kind
and restrained, but yesterday she could not control herself and needled me. She turned to me suddenly and said
with a wry grin, "And Lyova is at our house now." I
was stunned—he had been planning to go to a rest home
in the country. It stopped my breath, and tears came to
my eyes. Nasty Lenka, why hadn't she said a word about
it before?

I don't know how to help my friends—Lena and Grisha. It would be best if Lena fell in love with someone
else. And the same prescription for Grisha. . . .

My poor friends!

As for my feelings toward Lyova, I shall be able to
cope with them. Already now I feel that I can think about
him more calmly.

When I was reading the *Letter from an Unknown
Woman*, I was struck by one passage:

> I loved you silently. Only lonely children can
> wholly conceal their passion within themselves.
> Others will speak about their feeling to their com-
> rades, will wear it to tatters sharing it with their
> friends. They have heard and read a great deal
> about love, and they know that it is the inevitable
> portion of all humans. They play with it as with a

toy, they boast of it as boys do of their first cigarette.

Am I, perhaps, turning into these "others"? But Lena is the only person whom I can tell everything. With Grisha it is difficult to speak—he is writing poems about me and for me. . . . Heavens, what nonsense I'm babbling. . . .

August 13

Lyova is softly and imperceptibly slipping away into the past. Grisha has again become near and dear to me. . . .
Lena is away in the country. She did not come to see me, but she telephoned before leaving. And doesn't write a word.

August 14

Not a line from Lena. I understand that things are difficult for her. . . . But is that a way for a friend to behave? I must have a talk with her and try to help her. . . .
I think of my infatuation with Lyova as something silly and childish. And now I suddenly thought of Nastya, my Khvalynsk friend. What is she like now? Perhaps she is like Nadya, forever busy with tending her eyebrows, eyelashes, nails. I'm tired of Nadya. Much too crude, empty, foolish, and round—"like this silly moon in this silly sky. . . ."

August 16

Every day I get up with the hope of receiving a letter from Lena. Alas! She wouldn't even send me a line or two.

I am living nowadays without any unnecessary movements: home, Institute, occasionally the reading room, and that's all.

Needless to describe my anxiety. I could probably take myself in hand, but the general mood among the applicants who come to the admission tests groaning and moaning affects me too. The hardest part of it is waiting to see the examiners. You sit in sheer torture for an hour —and then in ten minutes you're done!

I have twenty-two points, and thirty are needed. Two more exams. Will I be able to get the additional eight points?

August 22

Today I shall learn my fate. I have thirty points. But yesterday there was a big scandal at home.

I was called to the director of the Institute, who began to ask me about my father, about relatives, who does what, and who works where. I told him the whole truth about father and his brothers. When I told them at home about my talk with the director, everybody flew into wild fits of hysterics: why did I talk about our relatives? Why did I mention my Communist aunts? I declared that I would never stoop to anything so vile as lying or concealment. And then everybody jumped on me—my aunts, mother, grandmother: "Brainless idiot! Hasn't learned how to live yet! Doesn't know that you must lie, that you must say 'I don't know'!"

My aunts are trembling for their hides, and I was nauseated listening to them. They want me to follow their example and try to make my way by "accommodating myself"—to vileness! No, my Komsomol honor is much more precious to me than "getting on."

August 23

Well, that's the end! I was kicked aside as unsuitable. And Sonya, who has only twenty-eight points, was admitted. Why? Because of father! And what an outrageous excuse they gave me: "In view of lack of dormitory space . . . " They said that to me, a Moscow resident who needs no dormitory space!

I feel so strange—suspended in a vast, monstrous vacuum. What can I do? Where can I turn? I keep feeling that it is all a dream—a nasty, ugly dream. In a moment I'll wake up and everything will be as before, fine, straight, and clear. Can any "practical" aunts be right, and I must really "accommodate myself," and hence lie and become a kind of tentacled creature, "an octopus"?

The sun is a huge red sphere. Or does it only seem so? It is setting now. . . . Everything flickers and doubles in my eyes. . . .

I am sitting here, reading, but now and then something unbearable stabs my heart, and I want to howl with despair. Why, why isn't it a dream?

August 26

Another quick review of the literary baggage deposited in my poor head in the past few weeks, especially since I am freer today than I ever was.

During one of our walks in Silver Wood, Grisha read Sologub to me. "This is the gist of the Symbolist program," he said. Sologub longs for another, mysterious, secret life, even if only in dreams, and complains that there is nothing but crude, rude reality. "In a Crowd" is a powerful story. Like Gorky's *Klim Samgin* and Tolstoy's "Khodynka" it depicts the mob—a rude beast that crushes, kills, and maims even for a few wretched pastries. A crowd, a mob—what a terrible thing! I relived the events of last winter, when I was caught in a crowd at Chkalov's funeral.

I have read a remarkable book, Vinogradov's *Three Colors of Time*. It's a very powerful, very expressive portrait of Henri Beyle Stendhal, the most intelligent man of his day, but unappreciated and not understood by his contemporaries. Stendhal wrote many books, but, to my great shame, I have not read anything of his. Keep that in mind, my dear Nina Alexeyevna.

The plot of Grevs's *The Story of a Love* is very interesting. It tells about Turgenev's love for Pauline Viardot Garcia, a famous singer and actress, and his meetings and friendships with Mérimée, George Sand, Flaubert, and Zola. But it is written miserably. As Gorky said about a certain writer, "he has made leg wrappings out of velvet."

The Gods Are Athirst, by Anatole France. A powerful writer, but I can't agree with his view of the French Revolution and the Jacobins.

My bookshelf has also been enriched by Mann's *Young Henry IV*.

And Romain Rolland's *Jean Christophe*. O-oh, but this requires a whole enthusiastic treatise—and I have not yet finished reading it.

In my present situation and my present mood, I read and reread Nadson's poems (and sometimes shed a tear over the page).

I still cannot force myself to write about my current state of affairs.

August 27

A crazy idea came to me today: why don't I become an actress? And I immediately had to confess to myself that I would be a self-infatuated actress. I frequently find myself guilty of vanity. I imagine everybody must have a mass of nasty characteristics, but hides them carefully. I imagine everyone has corners in his heart where he himself dislikes to look—it is so loathsome there. . . .

At the same time, each person has sleeping within him other feelings—strong, human, good—which nobody suspects. Often a rude, harsh man is tender and sensitive in his heart of hearts, and happy the one who awakens these feelings—he will be marvelously rewarded. . . . Generally, man is the most interesting object of observation!

August 29

I am going to Baku!

Unimaginable, outrageous things are going on at the Committee on Higher Education! All those who were not admitted to industrial institutes are herded into teachers' institutes, agricultural schools, veterinary institutes— in Alma-Ata, Perm, Saratov, and other distant points.

And then there are very considerable numbers like me, turned into lepers because of our parents. I met a girl who has thirty-four points (out of forty)! Her father was arrested, and she is also treated as an outcast. She wasn't admitted. After her father's arrest, she lived in the office of the director of her school (an amazingly brave man!), and did two years in one (ninth and tenth). And she passed her tests brilliantly. Yet we are constantly told that "the son is not responsible for his father." Such hypocrisy!

Everyone says I am lucky, being sent to an industrial institute in Baku. I could still go on visiting people and fighting. I am sure I would win out in the end and be allowed to remain in Moscow. But I've no more strength to fight. I don't look like a human being any more—a wet, bedraggled hen!

How will my friends react to my decision?

August 30

I am going! It's strange, but I welcome it. I will see new and unknown things, I will meet new people. My friends don't know anything yet.

September 6

Everybody knows the feeling that comes over you as the train pulls out of the station. Everything that worried and troubled you recedes, as though it has been left on the platform, and there is an immediate sense of relief and a kind of gay excitement. On the eve of departure, I was in a dreadful mood. I was sick of everything and tortured by thoughts of my second-class citizenship. I was tired to death of the good advice and kindly smiles of my aunts and pseudo-friends. But the moment I climbed into my upper berth, I sighed with relief. At home, the slightest noise interfered with sleep; here the wheels clatter, children cry, there is laughter and talk all around me, yet I sleep like a baby. Before departure, everybody warned me and scared me: watch your things, don't trust your neighbors, they'll trick you, they'll steal from you. For the first half hour I anxiously looked around at my neighbors and watched my things, then I gave up. Whatever happens will happen. And felt better at once.

Yesterday I could not eat anything. Today I have a ravenous appetite, and I look uneasily at my dwindling supplies.

My neighbors—Georgians—are going to Baku. I am a bit bored; they speak their own language, and I can make no more sense of it than of the clatter of the wheels. The window is open, but instead of freshness, we get blasts of dust and the hot smoke of the locomotive. The train rushes along a rather dull, monotonous plain, with here and there a wood, a village, a small station.

Before I left I received a letter from Grisha:

I wanted to have a talk with you, but nothing will come of the wanting—you and I have forgotten how to talk. And that is essential. I told you that I don't believe you. It would have been more correct to say that I don't know you. To "know a person" is to be able to predict his actions and wishes. And I cannot do this. I know only that we have blundered into a dead end from which we can escape only across a flimsy board laid across an abyss. If we cross it, the abyss and the dead end will be behind us; if we slip down, or if the board breaks—it will be the end of our acquaintance. Yesterday I wanted to tell you everything, but there is some barrier between us, and I could not speak. What was I thinking about? Loyalty to you. The feeling is so old fashioned that it might seem ridiculous. There was a time when I never talked with any other girl. Do you think it's funny? Perhaps it is. But it was then that I loved you. And later? Later I decided that you had stopped loving me, back in the spring of 1938. After that, whenever—chemically speaking—you found yourself with free valences, you turned to me. This hypothesis, which soon became a certainty, explained everything.

You have never told me everything about yourself, but I guessed it when your infatuation with Lena's brother—I believe his name was Lyova—grew into love. I think perhaps that I played the part of that "book of purification" that was kept by a certain German agent in France in Feuchtwanger's *The Paris Gazette*. You had about eight electrons in your orbit—this is why you have never been able to love anyone long. In Baku there will be new impressions, new fellows. . . .

As you see, this theory does not flatter you.

And gradually my love drew back somewhere inside me, assumed a potential form.

Then, for the first time, I began to talk with other girls. There are many nice ones among them. I liked Nelly and Valya most. We went to the movies, and I sat down near Nelly, as though by chance. At the Institute, I arranged to be in the same group with these girls. As you see, not a trace remains of loyalty. But, alas, this is not even an infatuation. You only need to appear on the horizon, and everything else disappears. Do I love you? The house is silent. The pendulum ticks and seems to say: so it was, so it shall be. . . .

The fault is all mine. I brought endless, impossible confusion into our relations. But I still cannot see anything clearly within myself. . . .

Those Georgians! Crammed themselves into our compartment from the whole car, drinking beer and singing. They are already calling me Ninochka, and asked me a million questions: where am I going, why. And a question which I have encountered until now only in application blanks: what is my nationality. True, my appearance is somewhat confusing. . . .

September 7

Today we passed through Rostov. By now I know all my fellow travelers. The woman is called Nina, and the Armenians (whom I mistook for Georgians) are called Setrak, Grisha, and Arutyun. They treat me from all sides to apples, chicken. Setrak is very handsome. He calls me "Nina-djan." The Armenian Nina is very beautiful, but her nose spoils it a little. She is very friendly, and she has a good, infectious laugh.

September 9

And now I am in Baku. From the very first step, everything strikes me here, everything is so different—the flat-roofed houses, the sea, the huge steamships, the people. . . .

But I feel sad. I feel lonely. I stopped at Uncle Kolya's. Tomorrow I shall get an answer from the Institute.

September 13

I am still not at school. Here too they seem to drag it out suspiciously, and time flies.

I visited the Palace of Culture and the reading room, and accidentally became acquainted with a girl student, Raya. I looked through her lecture notes and copied a few things. Although I am not yet officially accepted, I've begun to study.

But I have too much time, and I take long walks, getting to know Baku. Yesterday I went to Balakhany and walked for a long time through this exotic district.

Today I went boating in the sea.

September 16

The red tape at the Institute goes on and on. I may have to leave. Besides, the prospect of studying here is not too attractive—I'll have to learn the Azerbaidzhan language.

Today I went rowing again in the sea. There was a

strong wind, and the sea was covered with huge waves. But the sea, even the angry sea, does not frighten me.

September 19

They promised to give me an answer tomorrow. I think I shall soon begin school.

September 30

I've been at the Institute since the 20th. But this does not mean that everything is settled. They refused to give me a scholarship. These few days are crucial—in two or three days everything will be decided.

October 6

Well, my "course of studies" is at an end. Again I'm in the train, again the wheels are chattering about something hurriedly, harshly. There is something menacing in their breathless, angry talk. Are they threatening to crush me? Now they seem to reprimand me, and now to promise to improve things. What happened? I faced the prospect of living for five years—a harrowing thought—*five long years*—supported by my aunts! And, after graduation, of working in Azerbaidzhan for another five years!

And so I am going back . . . wretched . . . miserable. . . . Through the fog of the future I see only a single definite thing—I must work! Either in a factory, or in a geological expedition.

October 8

We are much farther north. I felt it last night, when I got badly chilled, and my neighbor came to the rescue and covered me with his coat.

Depression and hopelessness are rushing along with me, holding my head in a vise. . . .

Thanks to Heine. He alone dispels my wretched mood and sometimes arouses anger at those philistines who foul up the air of our homeland. . . .

Tonight I'll be in Moscow.

December 5

It's only in the last two or three days that I've begun to feel that I earned the right to get away from studying for a while and try to bring my thoughts and moods into some semblance of order.

When I returned from Baku, all hope of continuing school gone, I started thinking seriously about work. However, mother most decisively refused to hear of it: "You have a right to an education and you must have it. You will go to school!"

And yet once more I saw the flinty strength of mama's character. It would seem that no human being could endure all the ordeals and blows that fell upon her shoulders: papa's arrest, material privations, abandonment by many of those who had sat at our table so many times. And now, the suffering for her daughter who has been deprived of the right to go to school because of some unknown sins supposedly committed by father.

Mama wrote a letter to Stalin. She wrote about everything, and in the sharpest terms. "On what basis," she asked, "are they violating the principle that you have proclaimed yourself: 'The son is not responsible for his father' ? " And unexpectedly (to me!), mama was called before the Committee, and came back with a note to the Institute! I will be a geologist—my dream is coming true!

I was accepted despite the two months' lateness and given a scholarship, but with a warning: "You must catch up!"

How I worked! I didn't see the daylight! I haven't caught up yet, but the goal is already in sight. Everything is easier and better now. I needed help, a lot of help, and I naïvely counted on my friends. I thought: Lena will copy the notes, Grisha will help me with the studies. Nothing of the kind. Mama copied the notes for me, and Uncle Kolya helped me to do my drawings. And basically, of course, I was the one to carry the main load by myself. My friends did not see and did not realize what a difficult moment I faced in my life. Their friendship had been nothing but words, and when I needed help, I found it elsewhere. What I needed most was moral support, especially at first, when all the "sciences" rose up before me like a solid, impenetrable wall against which you could break your head. Lena did not even telephone me. "I was afraid of disturbing you," she says. Such delicacy, and just at the right time! And with Grisha it was even worse. I'd call him and ask him to come, but he could not—"No time!" And the other day he promised to come—and didn't!

I see it clearly now—everything is over! He does not admit it yet, but it is obvious. He seeks other occupations and diversions, he feels bored with me. . . .

In short, during the past month Grisha came to see me twice, and Lena once. Consequently, friends (such friends!) cannot be counted on in a difficult moment.

But the worst of it is that . . . I love Grishka! Deeply, seriously, in silence. . . . And he is withdrawing from me. . . .

December 7

Late evening. It's going on eleven. The weather—right out of Blok's "The Twelve": wind and snow, snow and wind. . . . As you cross the bridge near Gorky Park, you see the white snowy distance stretching along the Moskva River. Far, far away is a dark strip of woods, overhead—the powerful and at the same time lacy light structure of the bridge, and over everything—the heavy Moscow sky. It has a unique beauty of its own, especially in the evening hour when the setting sun sends up its purple and scarlet flares from beyond the greenery of Neskuchny Park.

Yes, Grisha, everything you said was true. . . . Grisha, Zhora, Lyova. . . . Life is so cold and lonely. Without friendship there can be no life. I look for friendship. I have no brother. Perhaps every girl should have a brother, to give her friendship and a brother's love. But, as I said, I have no brother. . . . To part and go in different directions, to lose the

best there is in life—friendship, love—you understand yourself that I will not be able to do it.

I have told you that life without you seems empty
to me. Not dull—no, sometimes even more gay, but
empty, devoid of deep, satisfying meaning. You
bring into my life something better than the things
people usually live by. You bring good feelings,
you bring the genuine essence of life. . . .

Like every ordinary person, I have many different characteristics; there is much that is good, and
just as much that is bad. You awaken the best in me,
you lift me above my own self.

Last time you insulted me cruelly. You do not respect me at all (not to speak of loving), and soon
you may even begin to despise me. You say of yourself that you are "a book of purification." Perhaps it
is so. Amidst the filth and rudeness of life you are
as an island of purity to me. I repeat again and again
that I love you. I love your dear eyes, your hair,
your clever forehead.

Mentally, I trace the history of our relations. In
fact, I began to live only in the spring of 1937. Since
then, all my best days, all my thoughts and feelings
have been linked with you. You have grown deeply
into my life, and it will be painful, terribly painful
to tear you out. . . .

What I have said to you applies both to you and
to Lena. Both of you mean the same thing to me.
Lena is also, though in lesser measure, a "book of
purification." And if I were to break, I shall break
with both of you. With Lena I get along more
easily—she is weak-willed, yielding. And all my misunderstandings with you are the result of our characters. I detect in myself a tendency to "take command," and you do not like to be submissive either.
We are both stubborn and self-willed, and I am
neurotic in addition (perhaps because of our family
tragedy). How, then, can we get along in peace?

All this makes me certain that the end is near, that everything is finished. . . . But I love you . . . and so there is still hope. . . . Speak to me, answer me. . . .

There was such a letter too, after a serious clash with my friends.

December 10

Yesterday I attended an exhibition of Russian historical painting at the Tretyakov Gallery, but have not been able until now to try and clarify my impressions.

When I was in Baku, many people (Armenians, Tyurks, Georgians) asked about my nationality. This question had never arisen in Moscow, and had never arisen in our family either. And suddenly people became interested in my nationality. And when I, a native Muscovite, was required to learn Azerbaidzhani, I began to feel with especial acuteness that I was Russian. Until then I had never had any particular thoughts or feelings about my nationality. And all other nationalities are the same to me—all are equal.

Last night, when I walked home from the exhibition across the center of the city, along Red Square, past the Kremlin, past St. Basil's Cathedral, I suddenly felt again a deep kinship with the paintings I had just seen. I felt: I am a Russian. At first it frightened me. Were those, perhaps, chauvinist stirrings within me? No, chauvinism is alien to me; yet, at the same time, I am a Russian. As I looked at Antokolsky's magnificent sculptures of Peter

the Great and Ivan the Terrible, I was swept with pride:
they were Russians! And Repin's "The Zaporozhye Cos-
sacks"? And Kotzebue's "Russians in the Alps"? And
Aivazovsky's "The Battle of Chesmen," Surikov's "The
Boyarynya Morozova," and "The Execution of the
Streltsy"? All this is Russian history, the history of my
forebears.

December 15

Every time that I approach the severely styled building of the Lenin Library, I am possessed by a strange
feeling. All that has stirred me, whether with anxiety or
joy, all the daily trivia and troubles recede from me, and
I enter the wise silence of the reading room calmly, unhurriedly, as though afraid of spilling a single drop from
a goblet filled to the brim with a precious draught, with
the legendary dead and living water which heals and
revives. . . .

I love the reading room. A stern silence reigns here.
Not a deadly, oppressive, or anxiously watchful silence,
but a silence of the mind, which disposes one to absorbed,
thoughtful work. The rustling of pages as they are
turned, the whisper of the librarians, the faint breeze
that rises whenever anyone enters or leaves. The quiet
of the reading room reminds me of the quiet of a wood
on a windless day—it is so deep that you hear the beating
of your own heart, yet all around you life seethes and
pulses.

I come here often, and take my place in my favorite

corner. A lamp, an inkwell, a pen, silence. The librarians know me by now and fill my requests quickly and efficiently. If a book is out, they will always put it aside for me next time.

Sometimes I cannot concentrate on a book. Then I turn to pen and paper. Now, too, I suddenly want to take stock of my reading during the past three months, filled with so many dark thoughts and so much pain. What a difficult time it was! I was made to feel and realize my civic inferiority because of my father's "sins"; then came the disastrous trip to Baku, the tribulations in Moscow, and that mad race at school. Nevertheless, my bookshelf has been enriched by a number of names.

Only yesterday I read (but I want to begin with it) Henrik Ibsen's marvelous play *Peer Gynt*, fabulous, fantastic, graceful, and somehow singing. You read and seem to hear music. I close my eyes and hear Solveig's song; I see the wooded mountainside, and a procession of gnomes, trolls, goblins, and the magically beautiful "woman in green." I dream that some day I may hear Grieg's music for *Peer Gynt*.

Veresayev (*Astray*, *Memoirs of a Physician*, *At the Turning Point*, and others), Pomyalovsky (*Philistine Bliss*), Sleptsov (*A Difficult Time*) . . . Alexey Tolstoy's *The Road to Calvary*—a remarkable book! Knut Hamsun (*Hunger*, *Pan*, *Victoria*). The proud Hamsun characters and their fatal loves! And his descriptions of nature! Lately Hamsun has sunk to fascism. I'll have to look up some literature on Hamsun.

Romain Rolland's marvelous books *Goethe* and *Bee-*

thoven. I recently heard a concert by the Beethoven Quartet. The music left a strong, profound impression. I thought sadly about the enormous gap in my education—no music. I rushed to get some books on Beethoven. If I am almost illiterate in music, let me at least read about musicians.

Boccaccio's *Decameron*. Let us smile and remain modestly silent about the impression.

O'Henry's short stories. People call him the American Zoshchenko. That's silly, of course. O'Henry is incomparably better, deeper, more original, and—most importantly—more intelligent than Zoshchenko.

And (how many times now?)—Heine. He went with me to Baku, he returned with me, and again he smiles to me sadly:

> How sad and how amusing
> It is to discover at times
> Two hearts that love one another,
> While the minds refuse to believe.
> Do you sense, my child, my darling,
> All the love that fills my heart?
> But she shakes her head: "Who knows
> For whom this love is meant."

December 20

I paid another visit to the Museum of Modern Western Art. There are many things here that I don't understand. Father had a good friend who was a fine artist. His name was Dobrokovsky, but we called him "Khudoga." Once, three years ago (he has also been arrested since), I went to the museum with him and he explained many things to me. Still, I cannot respond to much of this.

Why is Renoir's painting called "Girl in Black" when there is nothing black in it—it has every color but black? It is easier to understand his "Girl with a Whip," where everything white is done in rainbow colors. And Signac's "Pine" looks like a parrot. Picasso represents a farm woman, a little girl, and a drunkard in geometric figures. . . . If these are artistic experiments, it ought to be shown what these experiments have produced.

I liked Deni's "Polyphemus" and also Marke, especially his "Vesuvius."

On the whole, I went away dissatisfied. However, some people say that this should be interpreted as "unready."

Yesterday I went to see *Pazukhin's Death* at the Moscow Art Theatre. A pity I still know so little of Saltykov-Shchedrin.

December 28

Today mother received a present that made her very happy: the director of the Institute sent her a letter announcing that her daughter, Nina Alexeyevna, first-year student, passed all the tests for the first semester and showed excellent progress. He congratulates mama and the director of the school I had attended (the latter I surely would not agree with!), and expresses his certainty that she (that is, I) will continue to carry high the flag of an outstanding student.

To grandmother, this was a pretext for taking a drink, and to me, an occasion to buy a ticket to the opera *Helen of Troy* at the Nemirovich-Danchenko Theatre.

[1940]

January 2

We saw the old year out and welcomed the New Year in. Only the family was here—uncles and aunts, Stella, and grandmother. Despite the abundance of drinks, the party was funereal. Father was absent, and Uncle Ilya, after a few drinks, began to talk about his long months in prison. Some of the details were dreadful. I am terrified at the thought that my father may have had to endure such things too.

At dawn Stella, Lelya, and I went for a walk. The winter dawns in Moscow are beautiful. And this was the dawn of January 1st, when many of the city's residents were just completing the night. We fooled around a bit in the streets, and the star student did not fall behind her schoolgirl companions. When some tipsy celebrants attached themselves to us, we ran away with much laughter.

I fell asleep like a newborn babe, and woke only at five in the evening.

The year has begun. What will it bring? I have such a desire to study, read, grow. . . .

January 20

I love Moscow. Last night I had insomnia. I turned from side to side for a long time, trying to fall asleep. Then I got up quietly, dressed, and went out. It was after three. Silent, deserted streets, a fine, bracing frost . . . I walked without aim and without choosing direction. Crossed the center of town. The Red Square, the Kremlin and the scarlet flag over it—I saw it all with new eyes and with a new feeling. I cannot even define what I felt at the time. There are no words. What a pity I don't know music. Only a solemn symphony could probably express the emotions, moods, and vague images that took possession of me at that silent hour before dawn.

Leaving the center, I immersed myself in the twilit stillness of the Zamoskvorechye streets and alleys.

Moscow! The very word stirs me and fills my soul with pride, with the rhythms of ancient songs and epic tales. Thousands of years have passed over you, Moscow! Out of the ravages of fires, plagues, famine, out of the greedy paws of invaders and bloody internecine strife, you rose again and again, each time more beautiful, mightier, and dearer to the Russian heart. Thunderclouds are gathering today on the horizon. But can they frighten Moscow? Moscow may be leveled by flames, but like the fabled Phoenix, she will rise from the ashes still mightier and more fair than ever.

I am a Muscovite! Moscow is as my own mother to me. At times she may be harsh or quarrelsome or demanding, but she has always been and will always be a beloved mother. . . .

It is six in the morning. Lelya woke up, stared at me wide-eyed with astonishment, and mumbled, "Why did you get up so early, Nina?" And fell asleep again.

I shall also lie down. But before I sleep, I shall read a few verses from Goethe:

> Forever longing, forever dreaming of the un-
> attainable!
> But look—there is so much life around you!
> Our happiness is always near us. You need
> only learn
> To gather it by the handful, my dear friend.

February 24

Red Army Day was, in a way, the climax and reward for my Komsomol work this past winter. The District Committee of the Komsomol arranged a militarized march from Moscow to Skhodnya to Nakhabino and back to Moscow as a test of the defense preparedness of the Komsomol. I was appointed company commander— my company consisting of the students of our Institute.

The test mobilization and march were a success. My company completed the march as scheduled; discipline and political work during the march were in strict conformity with orders from the command. I received a citation in the battalion orders.

If war comes, I am ready for it. One thing is bad: I cannot learn to shoot well because of my nearsightedness, and I don't feel like saddling myself with glasses.

March 8

A cold, empty gulf is widening between old friends. I thought of Nastya in Khvalynsk. Something faraway and childish, but beautiful. . . . Long years apart have killed the beautiful childhood friendship. But Grisha and Lena? Especially Grisha? Love came to nothing, and friendship is also turning sour and moldy.

March 18

I am reading *The Enchanted Soul* by Romain Rolland. Thus far, I've read two books—*Annette and Sylvie* and *Summer*—but I am totally won over and charmed as once by *Jean Christophe*. Annette Riviere! *Riviere*—a river, in French. And Annette's life is like a wide, deep river, now stormy and seething, now majestically calm. There is great psychological truth in optimism: "I accept life as it is. It may be difficult, it may be grim, but I accept it—I accept its challenge!" This is the leitmotiv of Annette.

April 2

I am sick in bed. For a long time I've wanted to "have a talk" with my diary, but it is only now, when I am sick, that I can take it up.

I am through with the old. With Lena and with Grisha. And that is good. The fruitless game had grown too wearying. I told Grisha in early March to forget my telephone. He will not listen, but I am implacable. I part from my friends without regret or pain. Lena? Good intentions, never to he turned into deeds. Spineless, constantly irritated, promising a lot and giving nothing. I am tired of idyllic pictures and melodies.

The most interesting person in my group at school is Zhenka. He is twenty-six, a candidate for Party membership. One day he told me about his road to higher education. What a struggle it was!

I must rebuild my whole way of life and go on to the next stage—from school to the Institute.

April 6

I went to see the Chinese exhibition at the Museum of Oriental Cultures. The Chinese government sent many masterpieces of Chinese art to the Soviet Union for safe-keeping. Chinese scroll paintings, marvelous inlay work, porcelain, ivory, vases, fans, silks, robes, and utterly inimitable, astonishing embroidery on silk. And the lanterns! All this must be seen, it cannot be described. The two hours at the exhibition were like a visit to a fairy-tale kingdom.

It is now two in the morning. Silence. And I am reading Edgar Allan Poe. O-h-h! These stories make my flesh creep.

April 20

Attended another concert by Ginzburg at the conservatory. He played Beethoven sonatas. And I became convinced all over again that it is too early for me to go to such concerts. I understood very little, although some parts affected me strongly.

April 30

The most outstanding people in our student group are Zhora, Zhenya, Volodya and Irina. But they keep themselves apart. All the rest are quite low in their level of development. At one time I was interested in Zhenya, then I discovered that he is limited and rather lacking in culture. I would like to know Zhora better, but he makes no move in my direction, and, naturally, I will not take the first step either.

May 8

It seems to me that the best thing I've heard at the con-

servatory was the Leningrad A Cappella Choir and Boys
Choir under Sveshnikov's direction. The choir sings
without any accompaniment, but how powerful and
magnificent the voices sound! At moments you think you
are listening to an organ. I was especially impressed with
their "Echo."

May 22

Depression gnaws at me like a hungry rat. And I know
why: I miss friends. I long for friends. There are no interesting people around me. Except Zhora. But I can see
that there will never be any friendship between us.

I am nineteen. The best time of my youth, and I am
bored. Heavens, what gray, small people we have in our
group! And I shall have to live and study with them for
five years! However, am I any better? Probably worse,
but I am so bored!

"What can the Institute give in our time? Is it necessary, or can one become a cultivated man without it?"

"Only fools come to study at institutes. Gifted people,
geniuses, are always at odds with the mass. Star students
are mostly limited people. What the Institute provides is
not life, but vegetation."

All of these are Zhorka's aphorisms. Hence, he is also
a fool, since he is studying at the Institute? I remembered
the anecdote in logic: a Greek said that all Greeks are
liars, etc. But in argument Zhora is slippery and capable—
against all rules of debate—of tripping up his opponent.

May 23

The third copybook of my diary is ending. A third piece of my life. Every time I finish a book and have to put it away, I feel sad. Mentally I review my life—childhood and youth. How fast time flies. I look at my photograph of 1936, when papa was leaving for the north. An unfledged "ugly duckling" with astonished eyes—might be a Tartar or a Kalmuck kid—looking out and wondering at the marvels of life. And now I have come to the threshold of "greater" life and see a misty-lilac distance spread before me, beckoning with unknown joys, promising storms in its open expanses and sweet peace in some distant harbors. Someone's strong masculine hand around my shoulders, and a child's arms embracing my neck. . . .

But before all else I long for the storm:

> Brighter than blue the deep beneath it,
> And over it the sun's gold ray.
> But restlessly it seeks the storm,
> As though storms wash pain away!*

* Lermontov, "The Sail."

Fourth Copybook
Summer [1940]

(Pages from a note-pad)

He gently draws her by the hand farther and farther into the woods. Then suddenly kisses her cheek.

"What is it? What do you want of me?"

They are standing. Her hands are in his strong, hot palms. He lightly pulls her toward him. "I simply love you."

My breath stops, but I master myself and say, with a reckless shake of the head, "But I don't love you."

"It's not true, you're lying!"

"What do you mean, 'lying'? I say it, and I'll repeat it: *I do not love you!* I like you, this I can say. But love? No!"

"And I love you!"

"Well, then, love if you wish. But I won't."

He presses her hands and swings them. Heated after the running and the struggle, they loudly fling at each other: "I love . . ." "I don't love . . ."

Then suddenly they break from the spot and, without unlinking their hands, they quickly stride away into the woods.

"What a strange man you are, Zhorka! You are told you are not loved, but you insist on the opposite. How can you?"

"Because it isn't so."

The girl's heart is beating heavily and loudly, her breast fills with excitement: Is she really loved?

And the next day he says to her, "You're not offended at my drunken words last evening?"

A cold vise grips her heart, but she answers with outward calm. "Of course not. . . . It isn't worth talking about. . . ."

But in her room she flings herself on her bed and clenches her teeth with anger. How did he dare to insult her with his whims?

"Nina, what's wrong with you?"

"Go away! I hate you! Who gave you the right to mock me?"

"Nina, but I do love you!" His voice is troubled.

"You're lying, you're simply playing with me. . . ."

But her hand is already stretching toward his head, and she is all emotion and desire.

Kisses, embraces, tears, and joy—everything is mixed together.

"You know that I love you too. . . ."

"Is that true, Nina?"

"Of course it is, you nasty thing. . . ."

The days that followed were full of mixed feelings—happiness, and fear that this was not yet happiness—that this was only a mirage. And also doubt: why could they not talk when they were together? As if those two people who so greedily sought each other had no common language. To smooth over the embarrassment of silence, he kissed her. But she did not like this solution. She thought: they know each other so little. She must get to know him more deeply, they must draw nearer spiritually, feel close to one another. This idea gave her no rest, but he was . . . irritated by it. Physical closeness was easy to achieve, but knowledge of one's friend and of oneself eluded them. Their relations seemed to her unclean—all wrong, somehow. This was not love, she thought, but naked physiological passion. She tried to understand his inner world, his thoughts, his aspirations. And she received no answer to any of her questions.

"What is inside that beloved head?" she kept asking herself. "I don't know, I don't know anything!"

Uncertainty and anxiety stole into her heart. The premonition of the imminent end gave her no rest. Well, then, what if it came? She'd meet, she'd face, whatever was destined to happen.

And he was insistent, his irrepressible desires confused her. But she just as persistently shunned more intimate relations.

"No, darling, let me go . . . don't . . ."

"But why, Nina? I want you to be mine, from your smallest little finger to the roots of your hair."

And he caressed her with his strong, rough hands.

"Be mine!"

"No . . . I tell you, this won't be."

"It will! Everything will be. . . . If not now, then later."

"Never!"

This scene repeated itself over and over and left both of them exhausted.

"They all say so. . . . Do you want me to stop asking?"

"I do."

"Until when?"

"Till always."

"Well, then, until the end of the field-work period? Yes?"

"All right."

They parted reluctantly. And in the morning. . . . What happened? Nothing. . . .

Tomorrow he is going to Moscow, and he studies with Ira. But what happened? Nothing. He studies with another girl. Then they leave. And then? Why, nothing. . . . But I no longer went to see him off, as formerly. . . .

Then Ira comes back. She is in high spirits and most attractive—this always happens to a girl when something appears on her horizon. I feel sad. I can see: Ira is sorry for me, but she still refrains from saying anything. But I see everything clearly: he is no longer mine, he is with Ira. Is it a game, or something else?

Anger, chagrin, emptiness . . .

He returned, and it became still worse. They don't look at each other. He is with Ira. His hand often takes Ira's; they are together all the time.

A game, or a serious infatuation? But it's all the same:

he wouldn't get me to submit, he is only destroying my love and respect. Yes, I must get out of this. . . .

And so until the end of the summer practice months. Before departure he draws me into the woods. He says it's all my fault; why was I sulking at him? And then it seems to him that I tried to enslave him. . . . And generally, it isn't possible to live like that—just looking at one another, and despising everything else. . . . Relations must be normal. . . .

No-o! A man who is in love would not speak such words. What normal relations is he talking about?

"So you love me?"

"I do. . . ." But his voice is uncertain.

He loves me, but flirts on the side. No, she won't have this, she does not know how to scatter herself. If she loves one, the rest get no attention. This may be a boring kind of love, but that's how she is. . . .

September 22

I just read over last summer's notes, and felt sad.

Everything I dreamed of is gone: deep, strong emotions, sincerity in love. Something flared up and went out, like a will-o'-the-wisp.

And yet it is still painful to me, especially because we meet every day. He wanted to have a talk with me. What for? I've had enough humiliation. I have examined my feelings and know that I feel neither anger, nor envy, nor any sense of grievance toward Ira. I liked her, and still do. As for Zhorka, he and I are not suited to each other.

I have lately begun to think more and more often of Grisha. And I regret the lost pure friendship and love. And Lena? I loved her very much, and still do. . . . How good it would be to meet as before, and talk and talk. . . . But all the paths are overgrown with grass. . . .

September 30

Although it is a day later, the sonatas and symphonic fragments of Tchaikovsky still sing within me. Beautiful. A great and profound impression. Without knowing music, I am becoming a "fan." I run to concerts and operas, read about the great composers. During the past summer I managed to get and read books about Glinka, Franz Liszt, Wagner, Tchaikovsky, Rubinstein. Maykapar's *Student Years* is an excellent book. It gave me some idea of the musical world and a whole number of fields whose existence I've never suspected: esthetics, harmony, theory of composition, phrasing, the similarity of music and architecture: "Architecture is music frozen in a single moment, and music is architecture unfolding in time."

I learned about the "Mighty Handful,"* its history, role, and significance for not only Russian music, but the music of the world.

Why do I, a future geologist, need all this? It seems to me that one cannot be a cultured person without understanding music. That is one thing. And another is that I

---

* A group of nineteenth-century composers, which included Borodin, Moussorgsky, and Rimsky-Korsakov.

simply love music. As no other art, it carries me away to
unknown regions, it brings me marvelous dreams and
magical visions. In music there is movement, flight.
Architecture, painting, sculpture are static, something
split off from life and forever deadened. . . .

October 6

To my shame be it said, this was the first book by
Stendhal that I ever read (*Rome. Naples. Florence*). I
read it with great interest, but became convinced of my
own backwardness: the multitude of foreign names con-
fuses me. Honestly speaking, I should read it again—when
I am better prepared, of course.

October 8

Thanks to Paustovsky for his book on Levitan. This
biography of the great and original artist is warm,
thoughtful, and expressive. Chekhov was so right when
he said to Levitan on seeing his "Golden River," "Fresh
Breeze," and "Evening Chimes": "There is even a smile
in your paintings." How well this is said, and how like
Chekhov!

Paustovsky made me go to the Tretyakov Gallery
again, chiefly to see Levitan. I liked especially his
"Golden Autumn" and "March" for their freshness, their
joy in living, their blue sky and air. There is really a
"smile" in them. But two others, "Eternal Rest" and
"Still Waters," made me unbearably sad.

October 20

Reread Tolstoy's *Resurrection*. I detest Nekhludov, he nauseates me despite all of the author's efforts to make him attractive.

November 16

I was not feeling too well this morning, and went to the Institute only to be excused for the day. I was walking with my usual rapid stride along Kaluzhskaya, a kerchief on my head, looking disheveled and funny. Suddenly I saw Vera and Zhora two steps ahead of me. My heart hammered, and I quickly overtook them, turning my face the other way. But Vera recognized me and called out something. . . . I hurried away—faster, faster. . . .

Idiot! I mean me, of course. Haven't gotten over it yet, after all this time! Vera was in a pretty sealskin hat, a good coat, and he was bending over to her, saying something that made her face glow with joy. A rotten feeling came over me—as though I were envious. I am not jealous, no. I would simply like to be in her place.

And I felt still more keenly my own insignificance, my homeliness and shabbiness, the obvious cheapness of my clothes. My dear relatives often tell me that I am homely. Thanks for the kindness, but I know it myself.

Wide, bushy eyebrows (father's), a serious wrinkle on the forehead, ordinary eyes, a nose like a potato, wide cheekbones—my face. Most of the time it is serious—the eyebrows knitted, the eyes screwed up, the lips protruding. When I laugh, my cheekbones spread—a Mongol!

Who can become infatuated with such a face? As for loving it?

Grisha used to say that I am beautiful. That boy idealized everything in me. How far all that is now. . . . I remember our walks to the Moskva River. It was winter, a very harsh winter, but we strolled for hours along the deserted embankment, where it was, of course, especially cold. We kissed a lot toward the end. His kisses were shy, but passionate. And I never gave him an answering kiss. Why? I was embarrassed, it seemed funny and awkward.

And now all that is over. I have not seen him for eight months. My adolescence and early youth, my first steps in life, my first pure dreams are all bound up with Grisha. Grisha, Lena, beloved friends, you do not know how much I love you and how often I think of you!

With Grisha, there was poetry; with Zhorka, a heady fever, intoxication, delirium. Why did our relations break up so quickly? Because my refusals angered him, or because he became infatuated with Ira? But it is all finished. As I look around me now, I see nothing but grayness and boredom. And everybody disgusts me.

I perish in this slow succession of dull days. I long for something new, exciting. I love even examination time—a time of heightened effort, keyed-up emotions, energy.

The only person remaining to me out of the past is Nina Andreyevna. How intelligent she is, how sensitive, energetic, and alive! I see her seldom, but our warm, friendly relations have never cooled. We always speak about everything with complete frankness.

November 18

I had a long talk with Nina Andreyevna yesterday, and she described to me a rather widespread variety of scoundrels whose only aspiration is to "pluck the flowers of innocence." Zhorka is one of them. He failed with me, and now he seeks consolation with others.

But Nina Andreyevna herself is also on the brink of total catastrophe. Her husband was arrested. She feels crushed morally and physically, although she tries to keep going. She had to resign from her job, and she intends to leave Moscow to try to find a place in the provinces, among new people, and somehow reintegrate herself. With her departure, I shall lose the last friend of my youth.

November 30

The first letter from father, and what a terrible one: a special NKVD court pronounced him a "socially dangerous element" and sentenced him to imprisonment for five years. He spent more than two years in prison while under investigation. Twenty-six months! Yet it's astonishing how full the letter is of strength and freshness. To spend all that time in prison (perhaps under the same conditions as Uncle Ilyusha!), to be condemned to five years, and then describe with such zest the place where they had sent him for "reeducation." A wild canyon, a cold, crystalline, transparent, rapid forest stream. Papa was assigned as a work-team leader on a road-building project. His team consists of three former border-guard lieutenants and two workers. All of them either "dangerous elements" or "active Trotskyites," etc. Father wrote a beautiful description of the taiga and his comrades in misfortune. And he sent us a song composed in prison by a Moscow operetta singer.

I liked both the letter and the song very much, but mother flew into a rage. "Is he guilty, or is he not guilty? Why doesn't he appeal the sentence? Writes all sorts of drivel, and not a word about important things. . . ." She is planning to write someone.

December 30

Another year gone. It brought me a great deal. I have worked stubbornly—during the summer, the first semester, and now. I must become a serious, qualified, well-informed geologist. There was also social activity, which I performed with heart and devotion. And there was the heady intoxication of love. Only one thing was lacking, and is still lacking—friendship.

[1941]

January 4

On December 31st a letter came from father—like a New Year's present. It took a month to reach us. Papa was transferred from the road-building project to a drilling party which studies the terrain for bridge-building sites. He is working as a laborer. The party lives in tents and travels from river to river. His letter is again high-spirited and fresh. In answer to mama's scolding, he only wrote: "There is nothing to be said about my case. There is no case, only an elephant out of a soap bubble. I cannot refute what is not, was not, and could never have been. . . ."

And goes on to paint with rich, vivid colors the nature and the people with whom he lives and works. At the end of November, when the letter was mailed, the drilling party had moved in a frost of—50°C to a new river which is not even on the map. Before pitching their tents, they had to dig through a meter-thick layer of snow. Yet there seems to be an elusive, ironic smile between the lines of the letter. There was also another song:

> I live near the Sea of Okhotsk,
> Where the Far East ends,
> Without want, without grief,
> Building new towns for my land. . . .

The song is by an unknown author, a prisoner.

January 6

Yesterday I attended a Beethoven concert at the Conservatory. They performed the *Eighth Symphony*, the *Violin Concerto* and the *Egmont Overture*. The conductor was Nathan Rakhlin; the violinist, Polyakin. I sat, as usual, in the second row orchestra (and my ticket was in the first row at the other end, right under the roof!).

Strangely enough, Polyakin's playing did not move me. I looked at him more than I listened. But *Egmont* caught me up—I don't know how to describe it, but I wanted to get up and go somewhere; I had an almost physical sensation of flight, my heart was throbbing, it was difficult to breathe. I applauded with wild enthusiasm and could not take my eyes, brimming with tears of gratitude, from Nathan Rakhlin. He is a round little roly-poly, with a very warm smile. But when he was conducting, he was a titan, and his movements shook not only his podium but even the chair I sat in.

I liked the *Egmont* and *Leonore* No. 3 overtures better than the symphony. I don't know why.

I love Grieg—fairy-tale melodies, lovely music. It's all so dear to me. Listening to Grieg, I think of Grisha. . . . Silver Wood, evening, the rustling trees. Grieg creates a quiet, lyrical mood. Beethoven troubles you, calls to battle, to the ecstasy of victory. At times he even frightens me. . . .

And today I'll hear Bach. I still know nothing of his works. Will I understand anything?

February 8

For a long time I hoped to hear *Peer Gynt*, and finally my hopes were realized. It isn't enough to say I liked it. I am simply entranced. I sat in the first row orchestra (of course, with a gallery ticket again) and watched all the performers. Sharanova's nervousness, Tolchanov's interesting manner of playing—I could not help seeing it all, to the last detail. I say "could not help" because it interfered with listening until I lost patience and stopped looking at the stage. But *Peer Gynt!*

February 20

I've just read Thackeray's *Vanity Fair*. He has some pretty useful advice to people who want to make their way in society and be "good fellows."

But after such exhortations you want to get into the bathtub and scrub yourself thoroughly, with soap. Yet, alas, even in our society . . . The well-fed, well-mannered philistine is crawling out of the cracks in the floor.

February 24

Nina Andreyevna sent me a book: Lenin's *Materialism and Empirio-Criticism*. On the flyleaf she wrote, "To Nina, with the heartfelt wish that she will always preserve her directness and sincerity and rid herself of her supercilious contempt for people of lower intellectual development and of her mood of pessimism and passivity, which transforms the militant and active Nina into a benumbed 'sleeping beauty' with a certain tendency to whimpering and loss of perspective."

Thank you, dear Nina Andreyevna!

March 2

Books remind me with particular sharpness that, essentially, I am only on the threshold of the huge and marvelous temple of science and art. Every step forward gives me much, but also opens horizons that leave me breathless. . . . But I do not despair: every step forward that I take is chiefly for my own pleasure. I would die of wretchedness and boredom, or would become a drunkard, if it were not for poetry, for music, and for my books, if there were nothing but the dry cramming at the Institute.

June 20

I have long resisted the desire to write. Perhaps it was fear of a deep appraisal of my actions, or a reluctance to make things clear in my own mind. In short, it was the same as with my feeling toward books. I want to read, and yet, between the lines, I keep reading something of my own, something that stirs me more than the most interesting book. Before my eyes there is constantly a single image, a single dear face.

Pictures and memories of the past rush before me like tiresome "guardians" and "nursemaids." Light, surface thoughts float by. But soon everything is silenced, leaving only the present day, the present happiness.

There has been a tremendous change in my life. I am no longer "alone and on my own," I am "someone else's." It seems that my independence is over, that I will not be able any more to break away so easily, should it become necessary. The thread that binds me to this man is too strong.

Stendhal calls love a process of "crystallization." Perhaps there is much I do not see in the man whom I should know well precisely because of this "crystallization." But I like everything I know about him. His actions during these past days convince me that here is truly a Man, as Gorky defined him. Although I do it unconsciously, I seem to be testing him, and I would like still more tests, more difficult ones. I feel a need to be in Moscow, at once, without delay. On the first day of my arrival I shall be able to get a clear view of my attitude toward him. Moscow has often helped me to define my feelings, and I know why.

Here, in the countryside, in the midst of magnificent nature, intimacy comes easily and simply. Too simply, I would say. People who are totally unlike, who are worlds apart, are often drawn together, quickly and unexpectedly. Of course, this is an intimacy that is purely physiological and simplified in the extreme. It happens frequently in rest homes, or in geological expeditions like ours, where life is free and relaxed, with a minimum of cares. But as a rule these liaisons break up as easily when people return to their ordinary everyday existence, leaving only light memories. Of course, there is no rule without exceptions, and the relationships may be more serious. But the change of scene is always a test of the feeling, and may either end it or mark the beginning of a new and more profound emotion. This is why I long to go to Moscow. I fear, and yet I long to go. I fear mostly for myself: I know all too well my needs and my high demands.

I know that I love him physically. But intellectually? Only Moscow can help me determine. This does not mean that he must be a model of high intellect. But he must answer my inner needs. I must feel that he is a man who understands my thoughts and emotions. He need not like what I like or share my opinions in everything. No, but we must be on the same level. This is what I dream about.

I am afraid of going to Moscow. I am so happy here despite all the little problems. Yes, little problems! At another time they would have shaken me badly, but now . . .

I was just walking in the woods alone. The weather is gray, gloomy, with dark, lowering clouds everywhere. But the woods are always beautiful, and today they were magnificent: the birches and firs swayed under the gusts of wind, swishing with angry menace; the undergrowth bent to the ground, as if trembling with terror. And Koltsov's marvelous lines suddenly came to my lips:

As in bygone days,
Late at night again
With the coming storm
You'll have angry words. . . .

And you'll say to it
In a crashing voice:
"Turn back your rage!
Stay away from me!"

It will whirl around
Lashing furiously. . . .
And your breast will shake,
You'll rock mightily.

Wide-awake now,
You will fight the wind,
Whistling, blustering,
Rumbling lustily. . . .

What a pity he did not come with me. Ah, Seryoga,
how fast you have bound me to you! I no longer feel that
I'm "all my own."

He has given me no reason at any time to think badly
of him. He impresses not only me but everybody else
with his extraordinary decency, sensitivity, attentiveness.
My dear! I want to call him every tender name I know,
to say to him, "My beloved, my dearest! Press me closer
to your heart, let me sleep on your breast, my joy. I love
you, my big and tender friend. . . ." And hundreds of
other warm and loving words, to this man who is now so
fast asleep.

And the wind roars. Far, far away I seem to hear the
frightened scream of a locomotive.

I tell him the truth when I say, "I want a child." It does not worry me that I am young, that a child will interfere with school. I want our love to leave a trace. . . .

June 23

Do you remember, Nina Alexeyevna, how you secretly dreamed of experiencing great and stirring events, how you dreamed of storms and dangers? There you have it—war! A predatory black beast has suddenly swooped down from behind dark clouds on our homeland.

Well, then, I am ready. . . . I want action, I want to go to the front. . . .

June 28

How unlike this summer is from the last. Last year, in addition to all sorts of activities, I read a great deal, was interested in architecture, painting, music. It was a full, rich year. This year is altogether different. My inner life is quite limited; intellectual concerns have receded somewhere deep within. But in my personal life I am happy. Life is good. I love a fine, wonderful man. He is not only a man to me, not only a lover; he is also our friend, our brother, full of concern for us. He is loved and respected by every member of our geological party. "We are so far apart. Your whole background makes you ready for a broad and interesting life, and I am too simple for you." That's what he said to me. O-oh, my dearest Seryozha, you don't even suspect what a fine, sensitive soul you have. . . .

My dear, my lovely Lena!

If you knew how much I long to see you! I recall your dear face, your black curls, your voice, and your tender "Ninok." What a pig I am! How little I appreciated you. I long to tell you, Lenok, that I have never stopped loving you; there wasn't a single day when I did not think of you. I tried to convince myself: "It's nothing, there will be new friendships!" But I fooled myself—there were no new friendships, and there will be none.

Behind the window there is dense, impenetrable darkness. A new moon is being born. A sliver of a crescent timidly appeared and quickly vanished. And the hosts of brilliant stars trouble and agitate the heart like a great soundless symphony. It is warm outside. I would like to go out somewhere, to listen to the mysterious whisper of the woods, to glory in the breathless, immeasurable joy of living. And I have no one to go with. I feel sad without my friends. There is no one to whom I can tell everything about myself. . . .

The man whom I love, whom *I think* I love, is not suited for this for a number of reasons. And the first and biggest reason is that he worries about me too much. . . .

I must get away from here, my place is not here now. My place is at the front. Our life is shattered, it has turned sharply into new paths. One must make decisions and, above all, be honest with oneself—without cowardice, without hiding one's head from hostile storms. . . .

July (date unknown)

We don't know what to do. Hysterical telegrams keep coming from Moscow: "Continue work . . . ," "Wind up. . . ." And if we are to "wind up," where are we to go?

What is happening at the front is unimaginable—the Fascists have sliced into us like a knife into butter. . . . And everywhere—perplexed questions and shocked, puzzled eyes: are we so weak?

September 1

The hot rays of the sun stream down on the wide clearing. It's stifling. It would be lovely to take a swim. Then there's a gust of fresh wind. The woods rustle, shaking down the yellowed leaves, sighing deeply: "It's late . . . autumn is here."

Today is September 1st. By rights, we should already be back in Moscow, at school. But we are told to stay here, to finish the work, though heaven knows who will need it and when. . . . And the flames of war have spread across our land "from the chill Finnish cliffs to fiery Colchis." The enemy is already deep among our fields and woods. . . .

The future is dark and menacing. . . . But I shall go into this future, that's decided. . . .

The pale blue sky is covered with feathery clouds, the sun is hot, and all around me there are woods. I shall never forget the Tambov woods. Beloved forest! You were our friend, tender and welcoming, you shielded our

love from inquisitive, sometimes venomous glances, you
sheltered us with your dense branches and whispered
fairy tales to us. . . .

And the meadows, carpeted in early summer with
multicolored flowers—I shall not forget them either. I
braided the field flowers into wreaths and crowned my
beloved with them. . . .

The mowers have bared the land. Flowers and grasses
fell before the sharp, ringing scythes, and haystacks now
rise amidst the gray, desolate fields. At first, the stacks
were fluffy and aromatic. Now, washed by rains, they
have darkened and shrunk. On my favorite clearing there
is also a haystack—solitary and gloomy.

September 2

Our kindest Ivan Andreyevich, the leader of our party,
settles by the river, removes his knapsack, and proposes
a shashlyk roast. We rush to help him with joyous cries,
like small children. Ivan Andreyevich will be the chef,
and we scatter to collect firewood.

Half naked, in bathing suits, we run along the riverbank, gathering sticks and twigs. And then a large fire
flares up at the edge of the woods. And we, like a savage
tribe, are practically dancing around the fire.

Ivan Andreyevich treated us to some excellent
shashlyk. We gorged ourselves with great relish on the
scorched, smoky bits of meat, seasoned with sand. He
served me the shashlyk on the tip of a knife—all I had to
do was to open my mouth, which I did, like a hungry

fledgling jackdaw. Then we swam, splashed in the river, laughed at Ivan Andreyevich, our dear "guardian." . . .

But my heart turns, and mindless gaiety is no longer possible when I remember that somewhere, very near now, blood is being spilled, cities and villages are being reduced to dust. . . .

September 3

It is hard to say what is more beautiful: the tall, slender pines in the pensively severe woods or the gay birches, festive as a ring of peasant girls. I am closer in spirit to the sullen pine woods. One place in my woods, my domain, is especially deeply etched in my memory.

It is on the way to Kutlya, beyond the ravine near Krutitsa. There the pine forest spreads a little, letting a narrow road run through the gap. When I discovered the spot, it struck me with its beauty.

I came out upon the road and stopped, with a sudden ache in my heart. I was so moved that I burst into tears, and those tears were both bitter and sweet. It was a difficult time for me, but I cried myself out in the woods, in the shadow of the stern, listening pines, and felt the better for it. I was calmed by the majestic beauty of the woods. They seemed to whisper to me wise words about how good life is. Ah, how good it is to live! "Even in your pain and sorrows there is the joy of living! Don't cry, little human!" I looked up with gratitude. The crowns of the pines swayed lightly, and the road ran on and on, and no one was around. . . .

There was nothing but forest around me. All my

thoughts and all my feelings merged with it, nothing else existed. . . .

The two students digging below did not count.

Autumn is coming. In two or three weeks I shall leave you, my beloved woods, I shall go, I must go where the great battle is being fought. . . . And it saddens me that I shall leave my happiness here . . . to seek other happiness, and in another place. But I shall find it, I shall surely find it!

And it seems to me that the pines are saying to me: "One must live so as to earn the right to hold one's head as we do—high, proudly, independently."

"But such people are broken by fate!" the birches rustle, frightened. "Great storms break the proud, tear them out with the roots . . . be humble, bow down. . . ."

"Yes, but those who survive the storm shall be even stronger and more proud. . . . We sing our song to the madness of the brave!" I seem to hear these words in the noise of the mighty pines.

I listen to the voices of the woods, the solemn hymn of the gnomes and spirits. . . .

September 10

> I would stand arm in arm with a birch
> Watching the wind stir the leaves. . . .

For these words alone I would remember Grisha with a good, warm feeling.

Autumn. The wilted leaves are rustling faintly, circling downward, falling. The trees are turning bare, and a vivid, ever thickening carpet covers the ground at their feet. The pines stand proudly, calm and assured as ever, waiting for cold days and bitter storms. And the birches give up leaf after leaf, baring their thin, pliant branches. Every breeze sends their leaves whirling down. In the evening dusk the birches look heartbreakingly sad.

During the past twenty-four hours we saw each other only ten minutes, and that in the presence of the workmen. No, I must go, as soon as possible. He is so close to me, and growing closer and closer. And I am troubled by new thoughts, I hear the call of another life. I was not born "for sweet sounds and prayers. . . ."

September 12

The jolly fire warms my hands. I love fires. I watch the little tongues of flame, the curling smoke, and pictures rise before my mind, one after another.

. . . Scattering sparks, the fire casts a flickering glow at the huge fir. And all around me, the Pioneers are singing, "Brave partisans are marching. . . ." And the highest, the clearest voice is raised by Lyuba, the favorite of the entire camp, a wonderful girl . . . ill with tuberculosis.

And here is a Pioneer fire at which I am no longer a Pioneer, but a leader. I remember a night with my little ones in a tent near a fire. The Tartar boy Kolya, staring at the flames with his sharp, yellow eyes, sings a wordless, endless, melancholy song. Several "courageous" sentries are marching through the bushes, around the fire. Sometimes they collide in the dark; they're frightened, but they laugh. What brave children they are, and how proud to be entrusted with the task of guarding the unit!

. . . Every day—in the morning and evening—we lit fires. A few steps away flowed the wide and mighty

Volga. At night, sometimes, you'd climb out of the tent and sit down by the faintly glowing coals. You'd add some firewood, dig out from among the embers a potato carefully placed by father in the evening, and eat it greedily. All around, it is dark, the Volga splashes, rocking the boat in which father is sleeping. The tent glows whitely, beyond it rises a black mass of shrubs and trees, and overhead the stars are gleaming. . . .

There were many fires in the country around Moscow as well. Father loved to bring the family out to gather mushrooms and then to roast shashlyk in the deserted, silent woods. We would load ourselves with supplies and board the train. Then get off at any spot that pleased us. Whether we'd find mushrooms or not did not worry anyone. The main thing was the fire and the shashlyk. In the evening, tired, sleepy, we'd barely manage to get home, and straight to bed. . . .

Where, in what mountain gorges, what forests, is father lighting his fires today? There are no letters from him. . . .

September 24

As always, I come to the work site, and there is no one there. I am glad to have it this way—I want to have some moments alone. And I climb up a pine. High up, there is a strong branch that makes an excellent seat. And what a view from here! The cows are scattered over the meadow. The meadow is gray, dull. And the woods have grown darker. Only the pines are the same—green and strong. . . .

Do I have the right to live like this? I am badly

troubled: thousands of desires sweep through me, and thoughts whirl like a storm in my head. I want to go to the front. What meaning is there in my work, who needs it?

I must come to a decision. . . .

October 20

Fate and my character are playing merry jests with me. For two weeks I've been traveling here and there with a troop train. "Where am I drawn by unknown powers?"

I made my preparations to leave for Moscow quickly and decisively. The head of our party argued and protested, but finally I had my way, and he was compelled to give me a note that he was sending me to Moscow. Incidentally, Sergey was absent: he had gone to Gorky to prepare the transfer of the entire party to the Urals.

I came to the station, but it was no longer possible to travel the usual way. Then I went to the soldiers. The young sergeant immediately held out his hand and helped me into the car. And I started on my way. However, we spend more time standing than moving—now a day, now a night. And the main thing is that we don't know where we are going. They are waiting for orders from the command. Today the sergeant went to Penza.

I've seen and felt so much during this time that I could write a book. So much misfortune, so much suffering all around! The soldiers and I became fast friends the very first day. . . . Good, splendid fellows. . . .

October 28

I came to Moscow October 24th, and was badly shaken by my first impressions. It began with our apartment—I found none of the family there. An empty house. I walked, utterly lost, from room to room. Everything was in its place—the bookcases, the books, and even all the knickknacks: the photographs in frames made of pebbles from the Urals, the clocks, the radio (speaks just as clearly, and the same announcer as six months ago!). But none of the family—neither mother with my little sister Verochka, nor Lelya, nor grandmother, nor my aunts. . . . Empty. Quiet. A letter from mama on my desk: she writes that her office is being evacuated to the Urals. And advises me to come to the Urals too.

The empty rooms depressed me. I tried to divert myself and fight off loneliness with my beloved books. Alas, the dead silence was unbearable. I passed my finger over the bureau—leaving a clear line in the dust. I wrote: "Nina—Lena—Grisha!" And felt terrified—gooseflesh over my body—of the silence, and that writing in the dust. I quickly wiped off the words and went out into the street. . . .

Too bad I had not come to Moscow before October 16th! I would not have had to learn about the events there from "eyewitness reports." I would have been an eyewitness myself.

It turned out that the students of our oil geology department had smashed a large quantity of equipment, grabbed diplomas at will, and set out on foot for Gorky on the evening of the 16th. G. had a large share in this. She ran from one person to another and whispered, gulping with excitement, covering her mouth with her hand: "Moscow will be abandoned! I know it. . . . Moscow will be given up without a fight! We must get out!" And so—many got out. The Institute was deserted.

Oh, but the reckoning will come, you wretched cowards! Try to return! We shall speak differently with you then! Enough! You've hidden your rotten souls and greedy stomachs long enough with loud, flowery phrases. It was hard to expose you, although many of us have sensed the falseness of your declamations.

So that's what it means to bow to authority blindly and unquestioningly!

But not everybody abandoned the Institute. There is a new director in the office, and the chemistry department is intact. Good for them! But all the same, the staff and students will be moved . . . to be more exact, will go on foot to Sterlitamak. . . .

Nevertheless, there was much that I could not understand.

Why send away the young people when there are not enough forces to dig trenches around Moscow? With great difficulty they mobilize people from house to house for the labor front, yet hundreds of students, young and healthy, are being evacuated. What does it mean?

Outwardly, Moscow is the same, although the boarded-up windows in many houses jar the nerves. In some buildings, the doors and windows seem to have been forced out. A bomb struck the Moscow State University building; the heavy, massive shutters were blasted out;

the sidewalk is covered with piles of glass and broken brick; all the houses nearby and across the street seem to grin with smashed and splintered windows.

And on Kaluzhskaya, barricades are rising at intervals. Their fronts bristle with heavy rails, slanting forward. Antitank "hedgehogs" stand in rows, and behind them, walls of sandbags with openings for guns. Our beautiful Crimean Bridge is mined, and pedestrians are no longer allowed to cross it.

How my heart aches for everything in Moscow: the damaged Bolshoi Theatre, the ancient Book Chamber. I walk through the streets and think with terror: another ton of explosives, and this magnificent building will disappear. Perhaps it is the last time that I am seeing the Lenin Library, where I have spent so many hours in the quiet, pleasant reading room, where I have thought and felt so much. . . .

November 2

DEAREST NINUSHA!
I received your letter and now I am writing you. But what can I say? To begin with, I want to tell you that in your actions you are stupid in the extreme. I could beat you up for your obstinacy. I have always told you that you are still young, that you need the advice of older or more experienced friends. I am more and more convinced of the truth of this. I don't like to do this, but I feel it my duty to remind you of our talk in the woods when we last met. I told you then, as a friend, as a brother, that you are now at a dangerous period in your life. Be careful, Ninusha, I beg you—be sensible!!! We are living at a time when we must keep our eyes

wide open! Rashness at this moment is tantamount
to death. Be careful! As I read your letter, I cursed
myself for having been so unobservant. I am to
blame for your suffering, I should have prevented
your mad action. I want so much to be with you,
perhaps it would be easier for you then. You write,
"I have friends." These words hurt me cruelly.
How is one to understand "friends"? And who am
I to you? Don't you consider me a friend? Ninuska,
you nasty girl, what can I do with you? I urge you,
if it's not too late: take the first train going to
Gorky and come to the Urals. You must, after all,
have some regard for your friends and family.

With my warmest kisses,

SERYOZHA

This is the answer to my last "forgive and farewell."

Yes, it was a marvelous summer, full of tender caresses,
love, forest fairy tales, and promises "until the grave." . . .
He was away when I took my "mad" step. I left a letter:
"Don't feel sad, forgive me and farewell." I slung my
knapsack over my shoulder and strode away toward the
station along the forest path. I must go where my homeland calls me. And now everything is behind me—the
forest smells, the whisper of the pines, the merry dancing
birches, and the wreaths of wild flowers. . . .

Today I learned that Grisha is already at the front—he
went as a volunteer. How I would like to be there with
him, shoulder to shoulder. I remember his poem:

> Late autumn. Wilted, sere
> The leaves of lilacs and of roses.
> People have grown more sober and severe.
> Late autumn. Frost.

Yes, Messerschmidtts are roaring over Moscow, my beloved native Moscow, blasting the dreams of my youth with demolition bombs, burning down everything that has nurtured and nourished me from infancy. . . .

So this is it, my dear Seryozha. Don't wait for an answer from me. These are other days, and other songs. . . .

And Lena is not in Moscow either—she's gone somewhere. . . .

November 5

I walked a great deal over Moscow today, and saw a great deal. I was especially struck by one building. From the street, it seems intact. But it is only a deception. Only the facade is left, and behind it there is nothing! Behind the blasted windows you see nothing but the dazzling blue sky. Like a badly made piece of stage scenery. . . .

The days are full of anxious expectation. Hitler is marshalling his forces, preparing to pounce on Moscow.

I must come to a decision, and quickly. I cannot remain an onlooker. Of course, it is tempting to live like Flavius, the dispassionate Flavius of *The History of the Jewish War*. But the *future will not forgive me* for it! While I sit in my cosy room, people are fighting, suffering, dying.

The streets are filled with the clatter of the antiaircraft guns. Today was a beautiful frosty day, and the Hitlerites did not venture to disturb Moscow. But now, in the evening . . . there's the siren! The announcer is repeating over and over, with a special intonation, "Citizens, this is an air-raid alarm!" From the next apartment they are knocking on my wall—"Air-raid alarm, air-raid alarm!"

But the Moscow residents who remained in the city have become accustomed to the raids, and few of them go to shelters anymore. I did not go there even once.

Judging from the stories of eyewitnesses, many people have been killed in the raids. A few days ago a whole line before a store on Gorky Street was hit: people waited for raisins and got a bomb. They say the whole street was covered with bodies. But I walk around freely even during raids. In our district there are antiaircraft guns near the zoo and the First Movie House. The noise is pretty shattering, but for the time being it is possible to get along without the ear plugs that are thoughtfully offered to you at every street corner for the preservation of your eardrums. I sleep so soundly at night that I hear nothing. Many people envy me: "You have steel nerves!" They aren't steel, of course, but I refuse to stuff my ears with earplugs or hide my head under the pillow (like an ostrich in sand), and remain calm through everything.

November 7

And so, this is the day when Hitler promised to review his troops on Red Square. But everything turned out somewhat differently. Yesterday Stalin addressed us. We all sat motionless by our receivers, listening to the leader's speech. And outside the windows, bombs were crashing— it was so extraordinary, so strange. Stalin's voice sounded calm, confident, without breaking for a moment. In the hall where he spoke, everyone shouted hurrah and greetings to him. Everything was the same as in the past, except for the booming artillery, which spoke of the extraordinary character of our time.

Today as always, year in, year out, troops marched in parade across Red Square, planes flew, tanks rolled. Of course, I ran down to the center and watched the parade. I was especially impressed with the tanks. First came the medium, then the heavy, and finally the most powerful ones of new design. I studied them closely. Too bad I cannot draw.

In spite of everything, the streets are festive. The red flags flutter over doorways in the cold wind. Stores are crowded.

I am also celebrating. Yesterday I washed my laundry, scrubbed the floors, took a bath, cooked dinner. Borsch with meat, stuffed cabbage—not so bad, considering the time.

Unfortunately, there is nothing at the theatres, and I'll have to content myself with a movie.

November 9

Today there has been a particularly heavy raid. The alarm was sounded twice. There is endless firing.

"Tak-tak-tak"—clatter the ack-ack guns.

"O-oh . . . o-oh . . ." the heavy artillery is booming.

And now and then, infrequent but shattering, heavy explosions: somewhere a house was blown up, people are dead. Moscow, Moscow! How many years from Batyi's Golden Horde to Hitler? But never mind, Moscow is a phoenix. . . .

November 13

In the evenings, from seven o'clock on, the houses

stand like huge, dark, lifeless mounds of stone. They fill you with a deadly cold and loneliness. Cars move like blind creatures, tooting their horns in short, low blasts, afraid of disturbing the lifeless gloom of the canyons in this city doomed to grave ordeals.

When the alarm sounded last night, I was on Karetny. Somebody ran into the streetcar and cried, "Air-raid alarm! Get out!" The light in the car went out, and we piled out into the street, hurrying and stumbling blindly. Dozens of searchlights glided over the Moscow sky, studying it, crossing and uncrossing, gathering in sheaves. The stars of war flared singly and in groups, going out quickly. Tracer bullets spun long green threads across the sky. And the entire menacing picture was accompanied by the clattering of the ack-ack guns, the chatter of machine guns, and the pealing, deafening boom of demolition bombs. The streets became totally deserted, and I walked with tapping heels, pressing my handbag to my breast. And despite the shattering noise of war, the patter of the heels was for some reason especially distinct. I walked the length of Sadovaya and suddenly there was a frightful crash, as though right over my head—like thunder during a summer storm. I pressed myself to the wall of a house. A blast of dust and the stench of explosive gases and of something burning came at me from somewhere. I walked on. . . .

They say that the bombardment continued unabated all night. I did not hear a thing. As soon as I came home, I lay down, and heard nothing again till morning, when the announcer's voice said: "The raid is over! All clear!"

On November 16th I am joining a partisan detachment.

And so my life is entering upon the path my father traveled.

The Lenin District Committee sent me to the Central Committee: "You will find there what you are looking for." At the Central Committee they had a long discussion with us. Several people were winnowed out. Others left themselves, realizing the full seriousness and danger of the task. Only three of us remained. And we held out till the end. "This is grim, demanding, dangerous work," the Central Committee official warned us. And I was terrified of one thing only—that in the process of training and checking they might discover that I am nearsighted. They'll kick me out. They say we shall have to parachute down. That's the easiest thing of all. We shall act singly, at best in pairs. This is the worst of it. . . . In the woods, in snow, in the dark of the night, behind enemy lines. . . . Oh, well, obviously I am not climbing up onto a safe, warm feather bed atop the kitchen stove! And so, on the 16th, at 12 o'clock, near the Coliseum Movie House!

November 14

Oh, no, I am not flinty, not even hard as stone. And this is why it is so difficult for me now. There is no one around, and I am spending my last days here. Do you think that I am not tempted by all sorts of slippery little thoughts, that I am not reluctant to leave my comfortable rooms and face the unknown? Oh-h, it isn't so, it isn't so at all. . . . I feel so lonely, I need my friends so badly these last days. . . .

I walk through the empty rooms, and all around me

images of the past arise and vanish. Here is my childhood, my youth, here is the place where my mind matured. Lovingly, sadly, I look through my books, my letters, my notes, reread the pages of my diaries. And fragmentary quotes copied on slips of paper.

Good-bye to all of you—books, diaries, dear trifles that have been parts of my life since childhood: the inkwells made of Ural rocks, the stool and table in old Russian style, Khudoga's paintings, old photographs which contain the childhoods of father and mother, and mine, and Lelya's, and the Volga, and Moscow. . . .

I say good-bye to my diary. How many years now it has been my silent companion, the confidant of my sorrows, the witness of my failures and my growth, remaining with me in my most trying days. I have been truthful and sincere with it. . . . Perhaps there will be days, after the storm, when I'll return to your faded and yellowed pages. Or perhaps. . . . No, I want to live! It seems like a paradox, but it is true: this is why I am going to the front—because living is such joy, because I want so much to live, to work, to create. . . . to live, to live!

My Will

If I should not return, give all my personal papers to Lena.

I have a single thought: perhaps my action will save father?

Lena!

To you and to Grisha, my only friends, I leave all my personal belongings—my diary and letters from my friends.

Lena, dear Lena, why did you leave, I want so much to see you.

NINA

THREE LETTERS

December 8

DEAR, DARLING MOTHER!
I have not written to you for a long time, but, really, it was impossible. I have just returned from a mission, and am resting now. Soon I shall go again. I would like you to see how they outfitted us! Warm underwear, felt boots, woolen vests, mittens. . . . In short, there is no danger of freezing. In the place where I live there are many young people. There are many of us. I have not been home since November 16th. I had a sore throat from sleeping on the snow in the woods, but now I am well. You write very little to me. I returned from my mission and ran to see if there were any letters. Nothing. It makes me sad. Write me oftener, give my address to the family. Do not worry, mama darling, thus far everything is well. Kiss Verochka and Lelya for me. I kiss all your stern little wrinkles.

NINA

MY DARLING SISTER!
I kiss you hard, hard, my dearest pussycat. If you knew how much I miss you. Recently I saw your snapshot—your dear little face—and I burst out crying. The stern partisan!
I got many books for you, and my friends will send them to you. Read them, and always think of me. Don't leave mama, it is hard for her to remain alone. Write me more often, and don't worry about my silence. It is not always possible for me to write.

NINA

December 28

DEAR ANNA MIKHAILOVNA,
Please let me know where Nina is today. I received one letter from her, when she was still in Moscow, but then she became silent. I sent her three letters, but there is no answer. I am terribly worried. You know Nina's character. We, her friends, were always a little afraid of her flare-ups and outbursts. I am afraid that, with her hot head, she will think up something wild. Keep her from doing anything reckless and let me know her address. I shall soon try to get to Moscow and will attempt to find her. Tell her the sad news: Grisha, our mutual friend, with whom we studied together for several years, was killed at the front.
With all my best wishes,
Your daughter's friend,
LENA

USSR PEOPLE's COMMISSARIAT OF DEFENSE
GENERAL HEADQUARTERS OF THE RED ARMY
January 20

To KOSTERINA, ANNA MIKHAILOVNA

NOTICE No. 54

Your daughter, Nina Alexeyevna Kosterina, native of Moscow, died in December, 1941, in the fight for our Socialist Homeland. Faithful to her military oath, she showed heroism and courage in the performance of her duty.

COLONEL KUPRIANOV
Chief of Army Personnel